"THE LONG WALK TO DESTINY"

Mr. Ben

Copyright info
©Mr. Ben 2022

ISBN: Print: 978-0-6452132-5-6
         eBook: 978-0-6452132-6-3

All rights reserved. No part of this book may be reproduced or transmitted in any form or by any means, electronic, or mechanical, including photocopying, recording or by any information storage and retrieval system without the permission in writing by the copyright owner.

Published by: Wendiilou Publishing
Wendy Brown

Cover photography: Chimezie Ihekuna

Cover design: Wendy Brown

For more copies, contact the publisher
c/- 212 Glenburnie Rd
Rob Roy NSW 2360
wendiiloupublishing@gmail.com
0468 998 268

Scene 1:
FADE IN:
EXT: A DURBAN STREET - NIGHT
There is a playground with a sign, "Kimberly Children's Playground". YOUNG MAYA, 10, is playing in the playground, with other children. SAMUEL steps outside house, 5 houses from the playground. He looks at the children playing.

SAMUEL Hey! What are you doing outside at this time! It's after 6 and you are still here playing with those ne'er-do-well kids! My goodness!
(Beat)
Maya, I told you to stay indoors before I left for work! Here you are playing with them! I instructed you never to come near them, but you refused to listen!
(Beat)
They are bad eggs! Now, at the count of 3, go inside the house and wait for me!
(Beat)
One. Two. Three, and.

Young Maya runs towards her home. Neighbors watch Young Maya as she runs.

Scene 2:
INT: LIVING ROOM - NIGHT
Maya sits on a sofa and appears nervous.

SAMUEL Maya, you failed to listen to my instructions for the third time! I left for work at 7 am and told you how I expected you to behave.
(Beat)
In June, you'll be 11 years of age. You're no

longer a baby! You've reached an age where you should be able to take and follow instructions!
(Beat)
You were told not to step an inch from this house. You're on holidays. For Christ's sake, I expected you to read your books and watch TV programs.
(Beat)
But you chose to play with those useless children! Oh my goodness! Maya, why did you not follow my instructions?

Y. MAYA   I wanted to stay indoors but I was –
SAMUEL   So, you want to start telling lies! Who taught you how to tell lies? The N.D.W. kids? Those useless kids you play with, right? You're suddenly lost your voice. Haven't you?
Y. MAYA   No!
SAMUEL   Then tell me the truth!
Y. MAYA   I'm sorry, Dad, for what I did. I promise it won't happen again! I promise to always follow your instructions.
SAMUEL   I'm tired of your "I am sorry" attitude, Maya!
(Pause)
By what the wall clock says, 8PM is the time. Your punishment is that you'll have to write in this 20-page notebook the sentence, "I am sorry, daddy" 1,000 times. I swear that if you disobey me a 4th time, I'll punish you. Take this and go to bed. Before I go to work tomorrow, I want to see that you've completed what I commanded you. Get out!

Maya cries as she goes to her room. She looks back at Samuel. Samuel is watching "The News at Nine" on his LCD TV set.

Scene 3
INT: SAMUEL'S BEDROOM – NIGHT
Samuel sits in a chair.

SAMUEL   Am I actually playing the role of a father to her? How will she feel when I eventually have to tell her that I'm not her biological father? How do I tell the story that led to her birth if she asks me some day? In this life, anything can happen! Left to me, I don't intend disclosing anything about that infidel!
But how would she feel if I decide to tell the story of her mother's lifestyle? How would she feel if I told her that her mother was a jump-around? Am I really disciplining my precious pearl the right way? One day, she'll ask me where her mother is. How do I explain to her that her mother and I have been divorced since she was 3-years old? Oh, how I wish Cynthia and I weren't divorced! If we were still together, would raising Maya be such a mental challenge? God help me overcome this life's hurdles in future, I pray.

Samuel takes a sip from a bottle of vodka then climbs into bed.

Scene 4
INT: LIVING ROOM – DAY
The wall clock reads 7 AM. Samuel is dressed for work.

Maya, notebook in hand, is also in the living room.

SAMUEL Remember, this is the time you ought to be awake! I have trained you to always be awake at this time when you are on holidays.
(Beat)
But when you're going to school, you should be out of bed by 6 AM. I have to go to work now. Make sure you stay indoors and never ignore my orders again!

MAYA Yes, I will dad. (Beat)
Last night, you told me to write, "I Am Sorry Dad" on my notebook. I did, I have it with me.
(Beat)
You can have it.

SAMUEL Oh, I forgot! Okay, let me have it.

Maya hands Samuel the notebook. Samuel glances through the pages, which are filled with the statement, "I Am Sorry, Dad."

SAMUEL That's my girl! I want you to behave well and be the Maya I've always thought you to be.

Samuel pats Maya on the back.

SAMUEL From now on, are you assuring me that I'm going to be proud of you?

MAYA I'm the good girl you've known me to be! Daddy, I am happy having you as a father!

Maya has a big smile. Samuel hugs her.

SAMUEL I believe in you, Maya!

Scene 5
EXT: THE HOUSE – DAY
Maya walks with Samuel into the front yard. Maya stops walking and Samuel continues until he reaches a Cadillac. Samuel steps into the Cadillac. Maya waves "good-bye" as Samuel drives away in the Cadillac and Samuel returns the wave.

Scene 6
EXT: SCHOOL - DAY
"St. John's Baptist Primary School" is inscribed on the façade. Maya, with an Adidas school bag and a new pair of shoes walks to the school.

Scene 7
INT: AN AUDITORIUM - DAY
The children are led by drummers to their assigned seats. MR. DEAN HERBS watches as the children are seated.

Scene 8
INT: AN AUDITORIUM – DAY – LATER
The children are seated. Mr. Herbs approaches the podium.

MR. DEAN HERBS   We are glad to welcome you back after a 2- month long break. How was your holiday?
I hope you spent it well with your family. Did you enjoy your holiday with your family?
(Beat)
I believe you all did! As for me, I enjoyed mine. And I hope the same went for you, the teachers!
(Pause)
Now we are here to resume for the term. Class 5 has a new head teacher. She is

standing right behind me and will introduce herself properly when the classes begin. For this term, each class will have a total of 28 students. On my list are names of pupils who are members of Class 5 of 1991/1992 session. Our senior class. They are Spencer Hill, Makalele Thompson, Maya Isaacs, William Grants, Elizabeth Tate, Shan Craig, Tara Cole, Van Gore, Pierre Decamps, Maria Russell, El-Mohammed Raheem, Tanka Arawak, Bode De Silva, and Carlos Santana. I took my time to mention them because they are the "special ones". They are the ones you, their juniors, should be looking up to for academic excellence.
(Pause)
In the next two weeks, we will be calling out on this ground names of those who have yet to pay their term's tuition fees.
Therefore, ensure that you inform your parents about this so that they pay before or on the date.
(Beat)
The date will be Monday, next week. To avoid being shown the exits of the school, please, do not forget to tell your parents and guardians at home about this.
(Pause)
As I end the announcement, I want all of the pupils of Class 5 to march to their classes in a straight line. Then, Classes 4,3,2, and 1 will follow in a similar and orderly manner. If there are any further

announcements, your head teacher will

>   communicate them to you.
>   (Pause)
>   First, I will take my leave, and Class 5 will go next. Others will follow suit.

The drums SOUND. Mr. Herbs leaves the auditorium. The children file in behind the drummers.

CHILDREN *(Singing)*
>   We are going to our classes with clean and handsome faces,
>   To do as what we are taught,
>   For learning is better than silver and gold,
>   For learning, Is better, Than Silver, And Gold!

Scene 9
INT: PRINCIPAL'S OFFICE – DAY
Mr. Herbs and MISS SANDRA BROOKS, the HEAD TEACHER, step into the office. Mr. Herbs goes to his desk and takes the lesson plans out of a drawer. Mr. Herbs hands the lesson plans to the Miss Sandra.

Scene 10
INT: CLASSROOM – DAY
The students are at their desks.
The door opens and Miss Sanders enters. MARIA RUSSELL, 10, class captain, stands.

MARIA   All stand and greet.

The other children stand. The Miss Sanders claps her hands in approval.

MISS SANDRA   Please, do have your seats! (Pause)
>   This is my first time coming to this class. But you've made me seem like I have always been here. I'm so proud of you!

The students sit.

MISS SANDRA   Before I go into what we have for today, I would like to know something about each and every one of you.
(Beat)
I will call you out from your seat to where I am standing and you will tell the class your name and age.
(Beat)
I want to identify your faces properly. After which, you will return to your seat.
(Beat)
So, let's get started! Starting from you.
Miss Sanders points at Maya.
MAYA   I am Maya Isaacs. I will be 11 years of age two days from now.
MISS SANDRA   Great! That's good to know. I look forward to celebrating your birthday!
Maya sits and Maria Russell stands.
MARIA   My name is Maria Russell. I'm 10 years old.
MISS SANDRA   Okay.
Maria sits and ELIZABETH TATE, 9, stands.
ELIZABETH   I'm Elizabeth Tate. I am 9 years old.
Elizabeth sits and TARA COLE, 11, stands.
TARA   I go by the name Tara Cole. I'm 11 years of age.
MISS SANDRA   I like your confidence. I think you'll make a better class captain!
Tara sits and VAN GORE, 10, stands.
VAN   I'm Van Gore. I am 10 years old.
Van sits and PIERRE DECAMPS, 9, stands.
PIERRE   My name is Pierre Decamps. I am 9 years old.
Pierre sits and EL-MOHAMMED RAHEEM, 11, stands.
EL-MOHAMMED   I'm El-Mohammed Raheem. I will be

11 next month.

MISS SANDRA   It's good to know I'll be celebrating your birthday with you!

El-Mohammed sits and SPENCER HILL, 10, stands.

SPENCER   I am Spencer Hill. I am 10 years old.

Spencer sits and MAKALELE THOMPSON, 11, stands.

MAKALELE   Makalele Thompson is my name. I am 11 years old.

Makalele sits and WILLIAM GRANTS, 9, stands.

WILLIAM   My name is William Grants. I am 9 years old.

William sits and CARLOS SANTANA, 10, stands.

CARLOS   I am Carlos Santana. I'm 10 years old.

Carlos sits and TANKA ARAWAK, 11, stands.

TANKA   My name is Tanka Arawak. I am 11 years old.

Tanka sits BODE DA SILVA, 10, stands.

BODE   Bode Da Silva is my name. I am 10 years of age.

Bode sits and SHAN CRAIG stands.

SHAN   I'm Shan Craig. I am 9 years old.

MISS SANDRA   I'm the happiest woman on earth! Do you know why? I know that I have brilliant students who will understand what I have to teach. Again, I'm very proud of you all! I'm happy to be at the best primary school in Durban, and I am happy to be a teacher here. (Beat) And I know for sure you all are happy to be here too.

Miss Sandra looks down at some papers.

MISS SANDRA   I will be your Elementary Social Studies teacher. Let's go straight to what I have to teach you today, since we are short

                    on time.
                    (Beat)
                    I want you to take out you pen and notebook from your bag and place them on the desk.

The students take out pens and notebooks.

MISS SANDRA   Before I start to write on the board, I know you are wondering who I am. Yes, you deserve to know the name of your head teacher. I go by the name Miss Sandra Brooks.
                    (Beat)
                    You can address me as Miss Sandra. Having said that, let's go straight to what we have today.

Miss Sandra picks up a marker and writes on a board, "What is Marriage?" She faces the class.

MISS SANDRA   Write this topic in your notebook, and then look up here. (Beat) Today, we will be discussing "What is marriage?" I want to know who amongst you know what marriage is.

Maya doesn't raise her hand. Spencer, Elizabeth, Maria, Pierre, Tanka, and Makalele raise their hands.

MISS SANDRA   I can see 6 hands raised! The 6 of you will answer the question, starting with you. Spencer.

Spencer stands.

SPENCER   Marriage is the union between a man and woman, when they become husband and wife.

MISS SANDRA   That's a good definition, Spencer.
                    (Pause) Elizabeth, it's your turn.

Elizabeth stands.

ELIZABETH: Marriage is an institution that has a

man and woman being united for life as husband and wife.

MISS SANDRA   Class, give Elizabeth a round of applause!

The students CLAP. The applause ends.

MISS SANDRA   Your turn, Maria.

Maria stands.

MARIA   My dad taught me that marriage is a name, where a man is actually called a "mister" and a woman called "misses".

MISS SANDRA   I have not heard of this definition before. (Pause) Your dad must be a typical marriage counselor. (Pause) You're next, Tanka.

Tanka stands.

TANKA   Marriage is the meeting point where a man meets his choice of woman, only to be called husband and wife.

MISS SANDRA   You kids are amazing. You are the most brilliant pupils I've ever taught. (Pause) Next is Makalele.

Makalele stands.

MAKALELE   Marriage is a God-given opportunity for a man and woman to carry out his and her obligation to give birth and avoid immoral behaviors.

MISS SANDRA   Makalele, who taught you this?

MAKALELE   It's my mom and dad who taught me in our Church in Soweto.

Miss Sandra nods her head in agreement.

MISS SANDRA   They must be indeed Christian counselors. I am beginning to learn from you all, especially Makalele's outstanding definition. (Pause) Last but not least, Pierre.

Pierre stands.

PIERRE   Marriage is the togetherness between a man and woman to become husband and wife.

MISS SANDRA   Good! (Pause) To be honest, you have made me proud and my teaching very easy. No wonder the principal was very particular about your class. Give yourselves a hand! (Pause) Please sit down now. You've correctly defined what marriage is. Now, let's do a little activity. If you live with your father and mother, stand up.

Spencer, Maria, Pierre, Tanka, Elizabeth, Bode, and Shan stand.

MISS SANDRA   So, there are only seven pupils living with their fathers and mothers. It means that half of the class is living with their fathers and mother. (Beat) Okay! If you are living with your guardians, please stand up!

Tara, El-Mohammed, and William stand.

MISS SANDRA   Maya, are you living with your father or mother?

MAYA   I am living with my father. I don't know who my mother is or where she is.

Maya has an embarrassed look. Miss. Sandra has a look of regret.

MISS SANDRA   Class, please write down what I'm putting on the board.

Miss. Sandra writes:

"Marriage is the union and agreement between two people, primarily a man and woman. It is an agreement which is brought about by the oath of togetherness sworn at a special altar. This is to be binding by law and by the belief system the couple is identified with."

"Marriage can appear in the following ways:" "1)

Monogamous Marriage"
"2} Polygamous Marriage"
"3) Polandry"
"Monogamous Marriage"

"This is a form of marriage that involves a man marrying ONLY one woman. In this marriage, a man is only allowed to marry one woman and is expected to live with her for the rest of his life till death parts them. Christian marriage are typical examples. A Christian man is mandated by the law as interpreted as an oath of togetherness at the church's (or temple's) altar."
"Polygamous Marriage"
"This marriage permits a man to marry as many wives as he wishes. Provided he has what it takes to take care of the women he wants to marry, he is not restricted to marry ONE woman. A Muslim man is entitled to more than one wife only if he has what it takes to care for them all. This may include money, clothes, feeding, shelter, care or attention and time."
"Polyandry"
"This is a form of marriage that permits a woman to marry as many men as she wishes. Unlike polygamous and monogamous marriages, where men are expected to pay the bride price, women pay the groom price for the men they want to marry. This marriage form is practiced in Tibet."
"There are different kinds of religious marriages all over the world. They include Christian, Islamic, Hindu, Buddhist, and others. Religious marriages vary based on beliefs and rites. In Africa, the three most common religious marriages are Christian, Islamic, and traditional. A Christian marriage has to do with the union of a man and woman as husband and wife, using the Holy Bible, while the Islamic marriage has to do with the union of a man and

woman (or women as the case may be) as husband and wives according to the Koran. Traditional marriages vary, depending on culture."

MISS SANDRA   Oh! I have to leave early today. (Beat) Ensure that you copy what has been written on the board, read it at home, discuss it with your parents, and bring it back in the morning.

Miss Sandra slams down her marker, grabs her lesson case, and hurries out the door.

Scene 11
EXT: SCHOOL GARDEN - DAY
*Maya and the other children exit the school.
Some parents are already waiting for their children. Others are arriving at the school.
Samuel drives up in his Cadillac. Maya runs to his car.*

Scene 12
EXT: CADILLAC - DAY
Maya hugs Samuel.

MAYA   Daddy, how are you?
SAMUEL   I'm fine! How was school?
MAYA   School was fun! (Beat) I learned something I have never known before. It's about marriage. We got a new teacher and she is good! Daddy, she gave us an assignment that I have to discuss with you.

Samuel opens the passenger door.

MAYA   Dad, school was –
SAMUEL   Let's go home. We'll talk about it when we get there.

MAYA   Okay, Dad!
Maya and Samuel get into the car. The car drives away.

Scene 13
INT: SITTING ROOM – DAY
Maya is reading. Samuel enters and joins Maya. Maya shows no distraction as she reads.

SAMUEL   Very good, Maya! I am glad to see that you are doing your assignments. You told me you were going to discuss with me what you learned in school. (Beat) You also mentioned that you now have a new school teacher. I'm available to discuss with you what you've learned.

Samuel smiles.

SAMUEL   To start with, who is that new teacher?

MAYA   The name of my new teacher is Miss Sandra Brooks. But she told us to address her as Miss Sandra. She asked us our names and ages. It was fun! (Beat) We introduced ourselves. She was impressed at our conduct. Then, she went to the topic of the day, "What is Marriage?" (Beat) By the way, she is our new Social Studies teacher.

Samuel has a troubled look.

MAYA   Daddy, I wasn't able to raise my hand because I didn't know the answer. There were only 6 of us that knew what marriage was. I was the only one who stood up when asked if I wasn't living with our fathers and mothers. (Beat) Daddy, I want to ask you. What is marriage?

Samuel looks disturbed. He collects himself.

SAMUEL My dear, marriage is a point in life where someone has to decide to be with one man or woman for the rest of their life as husband and wife. (Beat) In marriage, you have to know how to live happily with your man or woman so that things will go on well as planned. (Pause) (Sigh) I'll have to stop here because you are too young to understand this.

MAYA Daddy, who is my mother and why is she not living with us?

Samuel looks around the room. He looks at Maya. Maya stares at Samuel. Samuel clears his throat and scratches his chin.

SAMUEL Maya, you see, your mom and I are not living together for some reasons that are beyond your understanding. Your mother, I believe, is alive and she is somewhere around Lesotho or Zimbabwe. (Beat) She'll be coming soon! In fact, sooner than you expect!

Maya is happy. Samuel is concerned.

Scene 14
EXT: SECONDARY SCHOOL – DAY
SUPER: "Five Years Later"
The etching on the façade reads, "Steven Beak Comprehensive Secondary School".
TEEN MAYA is walking with GRACE.

MAYA I have to attend a meeting to plan the inter-house sports for the spring tomorrow.

GRACE You're chief organizer of the school's extra-

	curricular activities. You participate with the Parents and Teachers Association. When don't you have some kind of a meeting after school?
MAYA	Today, I'm free today. You can come to my place after school. We can play Mortal Combat games and watch some movies.

Scene 15
INT: UR LUNCH EATERY – DAY
Maya and Grace are eating.
CRAIG, 19, tall, handsome, and muscular, sits with Maya and Grace.

CRAIG
Hi ladies. (Beat) It's good having this great opportunity to talk with you.

He looks at Grace.

CRAIG
However, Grace, would you leave us for a moment? I'm sorry for any inconvenience this may cause. But Maya, you and I need to talk.(Beat) It's all about our future. Yours and mine. I know you've been avoiding me since the beginning, which is fine by me! But I have to tell you what you really don't know about yourself.

GRACE
Really! (Beat) I think I will stay here.

MAYA
No, it's okay, Grace, I want to know what this man thinks he knows about me. Could you please come back in a few minutes?

GRACE
Hmm. Okay, if that's what you want, Maya.

Grace grudgingly leaves the table. Craig watches until she seems out of earshot.

CRAIG
I know you dislike me, not because of my looks or general behavior. But you seem

to hate me because I'm being labeled as one of those NDW kids so many years ago.
(Beat)
Do you know why we were called NDW kids? It was because we were told by our single parents about the lives of all the married men that lived in our Kimberly neighborhood, and how much better they thought they were than us.
(Beat)
Well, my single dad died years ago in a car crash! As for you, your dad was able to raise you because of an unusual occurrence. My dad told me your father was into many women, and that there is a doubt that he's actually your biological father.
(Beat)
You may choose not to believe it! But I tell you, someday, you'll get to know what I said was right! If you doubt me, go ask your dad who is your mother!

MAYA
Who are you to tell me my private life! (Beat) I thought you were alright, but I guess I was wrong. What my dad told me about you was right! I can now see the truth in what he has been telling me. Indeed, never-do-wells like you can't mind their own business! They go around creating confusion. Because they're hopeless, they want everyone on this planet to be like them! You can't influence me with your virus! Get away from here, fool!

Maya jumps out of her seat, scans the room and marches away.

CRAIG   *(Yells)* Call me whatever you like, Maya! (Beat) I love you so much. That' the reason I had to come tell you the truth. You'll come to me for more answers because I know you have loads of questions in your mind that only Craig can answer!
(Beat)
Your dad won't tell you an iota of truth because he doesn't have what it takes! I have a future for you. I am the only one who has a sure way to your being successful in life!

Craig scans the restaurant. Everyone is staring at him. Craig leaves the restaurant.

Scene 16
EXT: SECONDARY SCHOOL – DAY
Maya and Grace walk towards the school entrance.

GRACE   Craig didn't get into his early secondary school until he was 19. He joined the ALC.
MAYA   The ALC?
GRACE   Alternative Lifestyle Club, a juvenile organization which was set up to recruit teenagers, especially those from broken homes. (Beat) They initiate them to carry out underworld activities against humanity, such as stealing, drug trafficking and so on.
MAYA   I knew after his father died, when Craig was 12, he turned to drug peddling and stealing. He called them "hobbies".

Scene 17

INT: SCHOOL CORRIDOR – DAY
A clock shows 3:00. A bell RINGS.
Classroom doors open and excited students come filing out. Grace, with a glum looking Maya are the last out of their classroom.

GRACE What's wrong with you? Is there anything the matter with you? Are you thinking of Craig's words?

MAYA Well, not really. It's just that I'm a little bothered about certain issues I seem not to understand.

GRACE Cheer up, mate! It happens to us all. This world will always plague you with issues that you won't understand. So, it's left for us to filter them out subconsciously.
(Beat)
Let's go home, Maya! Remember we were going to play some Mortal Combat games and watch some movies at your place. Come on girl. Let's go!

Maya smiles and nods agreement.

Scene 18
INT: SITTING ROOM – DAY
Maya has her head on Grace's right shoulder as they watch television.

GRACE Where is your father, again?
MAYA He's at the International Management Forum in England.
GRACE Your father is a very important man.

Scene 19

INT: SITTING ROOM – EVENING
Maya looks disturbed.

MAYA   I'll leave him, never to set my feet here again, if he doesn't give me the answers I'm looking for!

Scene 20
INT: DURBAN INTERNATIONAL AIRPORT TERMINAL – NIGHT
Samuel steps into the terminal. He looks around. Maya isn't present.

Scene 21
INT: HOUSE – NIGHT
Samuel steps inside. Maya steps into the room

SAMUEL   Hello Maya.
MAYA   Hello Dad.

Scene 22
INT: DINING ROOM – DAY
Maya sets a plate of food on the table. Samuel step in. He grabs the channel changer and turns on the television. He changes the channel. The "African Channel" logo is on the screen. There are two people in chairs. The design in the background reads: "Sunday Morning". Samuel is focused on the television as he eats. Maya CLEARS HER THROAT.

MAYA

ON SCREEN
OFF SCREEN   Dad, there are a whole lot of issues that are giving me cause to worry. To

	be frank, I've been thinking about something a lot since you left for London two weeks ago. (Beat) Yet I am not able to come with the answers I need. I have this feeling that's it's only you who can solve this problem.
SAMUEL	What's the problem, my dear?
MAYA	Daddy, are you sure you'll tell me nothing but the truth? (Pause) Daddy, I want you to answer the questions.
SAMUEL	You know I'm always here for you. I've been with you and for you right from your infancy. I have trained you to be the sincere girl I've wanted you to be. (Pause) Why shouldn't I be sincere to you at this stage of your life?
MAYA	Dad, it's good that you are interested in hearing what I have to ask you. I remember when you told me that mom was away to Zimbabwe. (Beat) I can't even sleep for the questions in my mind. I'm seriously disturbed! Dad, where is my mom? Who am I?
SAMUEL	Maya, to be candid, it is a very long story. It all started in 1975. We were in our teen years. Growing up in the neighborhood of Gauteng, we had fun all the way! (Beat) Cynthia, your mother, and I started as friends. Later, we became lovers. One thing led to another and we became engaged. In 1976, we were set to get married when Mike, my now deceased friend, told me something was fishy between Cynthia and her so called brother, Gat. (Beat)

At first, I doubted Mike's claim, until that moment when I learned the truth. I hadn't the faintest idea that her so called brother was actually her longtime boyfriend, who had forced her to undergo several abortions. (Beat) Now, after such a long time, I would find out. (Pause)

Working as a secretary for the prestigious A & A Accounting Firm, she was always busy with work, so spending time with me became very difficult. I didn't know that most of her free time was spent in Gat's 3-bedroom apartment in Polokwane. (Beat)

Mike's apartment was a stone's throw away from Gat's. On the 2nd of July, 1977, I received a phone call from Mike, insisting that I travel all the way from my home in Pretoria to Gauteng to see for myself what Cynthia was really up to with her so called brother. (Pause) I boarded the next available flight to Polokwane and then took a bus to Mike's place. Without wasting much time, Mike took me to Gat's place, where it was soon obvious that Cynthia and Gat were having something going on. (Beat)

At first, I asked how he got to know. But he said nothing. All he wanted me to see was the illicit affair involving Cynthia and Gat. (Pause) I saw a car drive past us to Gat's place. We followed the slow-moving car which they were in, stealthily, to avoid unnecessary suspicion by either Cynthia or Gat. (Beat)

As soon as they went in, I initially wanted to

break down the door, but Mike was able to control my agitation. (Beat) We tried checking where we could find a place to peer in, to see what they were doing. Fortunately, there was a louver left open. Mike and I were able to spy on them through the open louver. (Pause)

What we saw in the next 5 minutes really surprised me. The woman I was going to marry was sleeping with her so called brother, a year before the wedding. (Beat)

She was engaged to me but here she was, sleeping with someone else! (Pause) Mike could no longer control me. I broke into his apartment, catching Cynthia and Gat with their pants down, so to speak. I remember yelling, "I never knew you were such a whore! Cynthia, you knew we were to get married next year. But here you are doing the last thing I would have expected of you! I can imagine the countless number of times he's laid you! You call him, this Casanova, your brother? You bloody liar! I'm ashamed of you!" (Pause)

I left the place saddened. I told Mike that I'd have to quit the relationship and move on with life. However, he told me to have a rethink about my decision, and once I had calmed down, I went back to my home with a decision to make. (Beat)

Do I give Cynthia a second chance or call it quits with her, in spite of my 3-year commitment towards making the relationship work? It was a big challenge for me! (Pause) The next day, I was getting ready for work when someone came knocking at my door. And who should be at my door but the lady I was trying to wipe out of my memory. (Pause)

To my surprise, the woman who had brought me so much mental stress was showing remorse. What could I do? I had to let her in. (Pause) Cynthia fell on her knees, begging me so tearfully that I fell for her plea. She confessed to me that she had been sleeping with Gat 5 years before she met me. (Beat)

She admitted being pregnant by him a countless number of times. Also, Cynthia apologized for lying to me, telling me that Gat was her brother. (Beat)

She asked me to forgive her for the wrongs she had sone to me. Cynthia assured me she would change. (Pause) After considering all that had happened and with advice from Mike, I decided to welcome her back to continue with the wedding arrangement. (Beat)

So, we reconciled our differences. Cynthia, to me, was a changed person. Or so she led me to believe. (Pause)

But I was dead wrong! She still kept seeing Gat, but this time, in far-away Gaborone, Botswana. What I saw on the surface was a changed Cynthia. Nevertheless, at a painful price, I learned that things are not always the way they seem. (Pause) October 5, 1979 is a date I will never forget! It was the day I went from being single to being a husband and, some day, a father. (Beat)

Things went along very well for a long time. Cynthia showed me how nice she was and seemed happy and faithful. (Pause)

Until I came back from work one day, only to see something entirely incredible! (Pause) Gat, now married and, by his appearance, a clergyman, somehow got to know where our residence was. He came visiting and Cynthia and I played host to him. He was entertained like never before. (Pause)

Later that evening, I got a phone call. My boss needed my attention to resolve some issues involving services to clients we handle. (Beat)

I dashed straight to the office only to discover, contrary to that I was thinking, that it was just a client's portfolio review he wanted me to analyze. (Beat)

In no time, I was done with what was required of me and on my way home. (Pause)

What made me go insane was what I saw when I got there. Cynthia being laid again in my own living room! All nude, Gate and Cynthia were so ashamed of themselves that they couldn't look at me. (Beat)

I didn't know what to do. I thought about going all out and beating them both, using my martial arts skills. Either that, or smashing their naked bodies with the TV set. (Beat)

How I managed to control myself is still a mystery to this day. (Pause) I pretended I didn't see them, went straight to my room, and took some documents from a file. These I took along with me as I drove off to go see my lawyer and friend, Ken, for a divorce. (Beat)

My ears were deafened to Cynthia's crocodile tears, and after I drove off, I didn't see Gat again. Till today, I haven't set my eyes on him! (Pause)

Two weeks later, the divorce papers were issued by my lawyer and Cynthia had no choice other than to yield to a divorce. Our lifestyle was like an estranged couple living under one roof. (Beat)

I couldn't wait for her to be out of my life. I was tired of seeing her come around and her presence generally irritated me. Though she cried all through, trying to seek my attention, I was hell-bent to seeing her leave my live for good. (Pause)

The time finally came, and it was the happiest moment of my life. December 15, 1980 was the date Cynthia and I divorced at Durban Magistrate Court. Shortly before that time Cynthia had given birth, a baby girl. (Beat)

The baby was some days over 2 months old when the divorce papers were signed.

Before we finally parted ways, Cynthia begged me to accept one request. (Beat)

"Samuel, I know I don't deserve staying married to you. In fact, I'm an infidel! Call me anything you like, I am what you described me to be, even more." (Beat)

"I want you to do me the favor of taking custody of our baby. I know you're such a responsible man and I'm just the exact opposite. I don't want my daughter to be like me!" (Beat)

"I'll forever miss you! They say: 'You will never know what you have until you lose it.' I have lost a rare gem. I will always love you." (Pause)

She handed over the two-month-plus baby girl to me and packed her things, boarded a taxi, and went away. I never saw her again. (Beat)

Maya, the baby girl is you and Cynthia is your mother. We named you "Maya" because the Hollywood actress of the '70s, Maya Priest, was your mom's role model. (Beat)

And because of the love I had for your mother, I christened you Maya. (Pause)

I think this is all that you should know for now.

Samuel, with tears in his eyes, leaves the living room.
Maya cries profusely.

Scene 23
INT: SCHOOL CORRIDOR – DAY
Maya hurries down a corridor. She runs to Craig, who is sitting by a wall. Maya sits beside him.

MAYA Craig, this is break time and I think this is the right time to discuss this issue with you. I need you to listen because to me it's very important! (Pause)

I know you were surprised to see me sit beside you because ordinarily you know I wouldn't come anywhere near you. But I really need you to do something for me. (Pause)

The last time you spoke to me at the restaurant you said something that really caused me to question my destiny. I went to my dad to inquire. Though he told me the story about when I was born and about my mother I wasn't really satisfied. (Beat)

He told me this was as much as he wanted me to know right now which isn't enough. Simply I have a strong feeling that he's yet to give me a complete account of who I really am. (Beat)

I know you have some vital information concerning me although the majority of what you said seems to be questionable. (Pause)

I need you to answer this question. Now that I know a little about myself, I'd like to get to know you and see if I could adopt your lifestyle.

Craig looks amazed.

MAYA	Yes, it may surprise you to learn that I've always admired your easy ways and everything about you. But I had to follow my dad's instruction never to come in contact with you right from when I was a kid!

Maya puts her hand over Craig's hand. Maya looks into Craig's eyes.

MAYA	Sincerely, I looked forward to expressing this feeling towards you. I think my association with you will make me find out the complete truth about myself! (Beat) To be candid, I want to know who you really are Craig!
CRAIG	This is the greatest day of my life! (Beat) The girl whom I thought never had a single regard for me had all this while privately loved me from the get go!

Craig puts an arm around Maya's shoulders.

CRAIG	Well, it's a great honor knowing that you love me the same way I love you! And I'd be glad to let you know what makes me different from all of my peers. Or perhaps, I should say "who".

Maya has a surprised look. Craig Smiles.

CRAIG	Without wasting much time, I'll introduce you to her. She'll tell you what to do to reach your destiny. To uncover the complete truth about who you really are. (Beat) But I have to warn you, this information will come at a price. Are you sure you're ready for all this?
MAYA	I'll do what it takes to find my destiny, even if it means putting my life on the line!
CRAIG	Go that! (Beat) I'll take you to her office tomorrow. (Pause) However, there's one more thing, Maya. I want you to agree with me this moment. You'll have to be my girl.

Maya pauses then looks into Craig's eyes.

MAYA	I will.

Scene 24

INT: INDUSTRIAL PARK – DAY TRACKING
Craig leads Maya by office doors.

CRAIG My mother left home when I was 3. My father died in an accident when I was 12. (Beat) When I was 19, I was being chased by hoodlums. This woman was driving by. She stopped, told me to get in the car. When I got in, she sped away. (Beat) She enrolled me in the Steven Beak Comprehensive School.

MAYA I can see why you're loyal to her.

Craig stops at an office door with a small window. Maya peers inside the office.

Scene 25
INT: MS. DIANA'S OFFICE – DAY
Craig leads Maya inside.
There are cardboard posters from many different countries. Some show artifacts and other show world events. Other posters have quotes from famous people.
There was a mini-sized refrigerator in a corner by the exit. There is a large sofa.
Three sides of Ms. Diana's executive desk had chairs. She sat in a large, upholstered chair. She is gaily dressed. She is going through some paperwork.

MAYA What are we doing here?
CRAIG Ms. Diana is the woman I told you about. The one who will help you reach your destiny.
MAYA Really? I thought she was just a brand- new teacher here.
MS. DIANA Come in.
Ms. Diana stands.

MS. DIANA　　　How you doing, Craig?

She gestures to the chairs at her desk.

MS. DIANA　　　Please, have a seat.

CRAIG　　　No problem, madam.

MS. DIANA　　　Now, to what do I owe the pleasure of this visit, Craig?

CRAIG　　　I've come in to give you what you've always requested.

MS. DIANA　　　Mr. Craig, what could that be?

CRAIG　　　Okay, for the sake of formality, I want you to know that I've brought a prospect, willing to join your pursuit. She goes by the name Maya Isaacs, and she is in her 2nd year of her senior secondary school.

MS. DIANA　　　Yes, I know who she is.

Ms. Diana flashes a warm smile at Maya. Craig nods.

CRAIG　　　She has been trying so hard to find her destiny. In fact, she told me she'd do all it takes to accomplish her desire in life! She has wanted to know who her identity is. (Beat)
But her father wouldn't disclose it completely. I strongly feel, just as she does, that her father is denying her the right to information because he feels she's too young to know things! (Beat)
She also wanted to know what makes me unique from my peers in this school. These are the reasons we're here.

Ms. Diana sits and leans back in her chair apparently satisfied with the explanation.

MS. DIANA　　　Now I fully understand what you've said, Craig. It's good to know that there are people in this part of the world who will do all it takes to get what they want.

Ms. Diana has a sad look as she nods.

MS. DIANA I can believe that parents these days are still sticking to the old-fashioned way of training their children!

Ms. Diana turns to Maya.

MS. DIANA I want to confirm all that Craig has said about you, Maya. To begin with, Craig told me you go by the name Maya Isaacs, right?

MAYA Yes.

MS. DIANA He mentioned that you are in search of your true identity.

MAYA He' right

MS. DIANA Who are you living with, your dad or your mom?

MAYA I live with my dad. They are divorced.

MS. DIANA Why the look on your face? Don't tell me this question got to you! If yes, I'll stop questioning you.

MAYA It's nothing, really. Don't mind me. You can go ahead.

maya chuckles.

MS. DIANA Do you think you have what it takes to be part of my pursuit?

MAYA Like Craig said, I'm ready to give it all it takes, provided this pursuit will provide for me what I desire!

MS. DIANA That's the spirit!

Ms. Diana stands.

MS. DIANA This is the very quality I've been looking for in juveniles like you. I'm happy my ambition has been achieved.

Ms. Diana walks around the table and puts a hand on

Maya's shoulder.

MS. DIANA   I've been looking for just one more initiate these past 7 years, to finish getting the 39 members needed for my all- juvenile organization. We are aimed at giving people the lifestyle they never ha by living with their parents. (Whispering) I'm not really a teacher per se. I just used this as a front to look for that initiate who will complete the compulsory 39-member arrangement. (Beat)

From the way I see it, Maya, you are already the lucky one, although you have to complete the initiation rites and observe other activities that will follow. (Beat)

Your membership will come at a price. I know you have what it takes to be a full-fledged member of my organization. (Laughs) Don't be afraid! Craig and 13 other students of this school have been initiated. You'll get to meet them all. Indeed, they are happy that they are now a part of my pursuit. (Beat)

The moment I have you as the 39th member, I'll tender my resignation as a teacher! (Pause) With that being said, I want to give Craig what I promised him. (Beat)

Craig, come see me personally in the office tomorrow for your money. Well done!
(To Maya)
Before you leave my office, I'd like you to fill out your name, phone number, and home address for me. Plus, I need to take a picture of you. Tomorrow, we'll head to the

      initiation ground at the prestigious La Pierre Hotel at the heart of Durban.

Ms. Diana escorts Craig and Maya to the door.

MS. DIANA Nothing will happen to you. Again, don't be afraid! All I need from you is your availability. Come to school in your uniform, as you usually do, and after the assembly, come see me at my office.

Maya writes on a pad and gives it to Ms. Diana. Ms. Diana snaps a picture of Maya. Ms. Diana shakes hands with Craig.

Scene 26
EXT: MS. DIANA'S OFFICE – DAY
Everyone is smiling as they leave the office. They go in three different directions.

Scene 27
INT: HOUSE – DAY
Maya is all smiles when she comes home.

Scene 28
INT: MAYA'S ROOM – NIGHT
Maya is excited.

Scene 29
INT: KITCHEN – NIGHT
The oven clock shows it's 5 AM.
Samuel comes into the kitchen and appears favorably impressed.

Scene 30
INT: MS. DIANA'S OFFICE – DAY
Ms. Diana hands some money to Craig. Maya opens the

door. Craig shoves the money into his pocket.
MS. DIANA   It's good to see you!
Ms. Diana hugs Maya. Craig arranges some of Ms. Diana's personal effects.
MS. DIANA   How was your night?
MAYA   Very great, Ms. Diana.
Ms. Diana glances at a wall clock.
MS. DIANA   Guys, it's about time we left this place. (Beat) If you observed carefully on your way to school, you will have seen that there was a bus next to the school, with "The Alternative Lifestyle Club" written on its side. (Beat)
There are other members already on it. That bus will take us straight to the Club. Craig and I have been in the office since before 6 a.m., waiting for you. (Pause)
We have to avoid being seen by any staff or student of the school. Six a.m. is the right time for this, and no later! Now that you're here, I think we should leave for the La Pierre Hotel. (Beat) Shouldn't we, Craig?
CRAIG   From the look of things, I think you're right. We have to leave now! (Beat) Time is of the essence. We have to leave this place before the school's 7 a.m. working hour.
MS. DIANA   Let's go then!
She ushers Craig and Maya out of the office. She locks the door and the trio hurry away.

Scene 31
EXT: SECONDARY SCHOOL - DAY
A bus with The Alternative Lifestyle Club" written on its side is in front of the school. Craig, Maya, and Ms. Diana

run to the bus and board it.

Scene 32
INT: BUS - DRIVING - DAY
Ms. Diana sits in front.
Maya is seated with the others on the full bus. The La Pierre Hotel is outside the bus. The bus stops.

Scene 33
INT: UNDERGROUND FACILITY - DAY
Maya appears nervous.
The walls have pictures of young men and women carrying human skulls. Another picture depicts a sex orgy.

Scene 34
INT: RED ROOM - DAY
A large room with red walls. There is what looks like a throne at the far end of the room. There is a bucket with a reddish liquid near a wall. The group files inside.
Maya appears frightened. Ms. Diana enters, looking like something out of "The Samurai Goddess".
Maya, and the others, are perspiring and shaking. Ms. Diana walks to the bucket.

MS. DIANA   Form two lines!
She points out two places.
MS. DIANA   Half here and half here.
The move to form the lines.
MS. DIANA   Face each other.
She waits as the two lines are formed.
MS. DIANA   The Great Alternative Lifestyle Club!
GROUP   We live our lives for the Club!
Maya quivering but determined.
MS. DIANA   We are here to give life to all juveniles

around the world, a life that they would ordinarily not have with their parents of guardians. (Beat)

This is the vision of the Alternative Lifestyle Club. It started in 1978 as a book, written by the late Dr. Steven Micah, who later became the country's Minister of Finance. (Beat)

However, the book was not published until 1991, under the auspices of the late Miriam Song, wife of the country's former minister of Power and Steel, Mr. Henry Song. (Pause) She followed the dictates of the club, powerfully written in the book, whereby she has to get only 39 members for this assembly to begin and flourish. (Beat)

To the ALC, "39" is a very sacred number, because it takes the juvenile energy 3 tries to attain the highest feats we desire, which is placed at 13. (Beat)

In theory, I mean it would take the product of the number "3" of the earth's energy field reflected in a juvenile, and the highest secular number, 13, to achieve our vision and mission. (Beat)

Before I conclude, and begin with the initiation proper, I would like to make the goal of the ALC clear. (Beat)

The mission of the ALC is to recruit juveniles, especially at college and secondary school levels, to spread its gospel to all parts of Africa and other parts of the world, starting with the Republic of South Africa. (Pause)

Let's remind ourselves of the Seven Point

	Creed, or what we call the ALC's gospel.
GROUP	One. All juveniles have the right to do as they wish, because they are growing into adults. (Pause) Two. All young people are to experiment with what gives them fulfillment, provided they are approved by the ALC. (Pause) Three. All young people deserve the right to adhere to what the system has to tell them. (Pause) Four. The ALC is the best assembly for all juveniles in the world. (Pause)
	Five. We give opportunities to our members that some grown men and women would never have. (Pause) Six. What we do is targeted at two Ps, pressure and pain. The pressure sassociated with carrying out ALC's responsibilities, the underworld activities of stealing, robbery, and prostitution, mount as the pains surface to give birth to the rights or gains that its members enjoy.

Ms. Diana smiles at Maya.

MS. DIANA	ALC now has a member in the making. Craig told me that her name is Maya Isaacs. According to him, she is in search of her destiny, and wants to know her true identity. (Beat)
	It's good that she came to the right place! Craig, bring her here so that the initiate rites can commence.

Craig brings Maya to Ms. Diana.

MAYA	Before moving further, young girl, I would like to confirm a few bits of information. I need nothing but your sincere answers.

Ms. Diana gives a fierce look. Maya is terrified.

MS. DIANA   You gave your name as Maya Isaacs, right?

MAYA   (Stutters) Yes.

MS. DIANA   I was informed that you are 15 years old. It this right?

MAYA   (Stutters) Yes.

MS. DIANA   You want to identify who you are. You really want to know who and what you are. The search for your destiny. Am I correct?

MAYA   Yes.

MS. DIANA   You told me you have the heart to join us.

MAYA   Yes.

MS. DIANA   Maya, do you know what the initiation will entail? Do you know the price you will have to pay?

MAYA   No, no.

MS. DIANA   You told me you were living with your father. He is divorced, right?

MAYA   Yes, yes, he and my mother are divorced.

MS. DIANA   Are you a virgin?

Maya looks down.

MAYA   Yes, I am.

MS. DIANA   I knew you were the right person to make this organization complete. (Beat) Well, you will have to undergo a rite known as Sexual Unveiling. This will involve Craig, the person who introduced you to me. He will sexually defile you and make you realize the other side of feminine energy. (Beat)
After doing this to you for hours in the

presence of all the initiates, I will pour the liquid in this bucket on your body.

Maya tries to run but Craig holds her tight. Ms. Diana nods at Craig.

MS. DIANA   You will then be bathed by all the initiates in my presence with this ancient Chinese soap. After the process, you'll put round your neck the ALC chain, just like you are seeing all of us wearing. (Beat)

Then, you'll receive the manual of information that gives you the right to do as you wish, experiment with what gives you pleasure like sex, and have a thorough knowledge of good and evil, among other things. (Pause)

But you would have to ensure that you separate completely from your father. We will be sending you on various operations through Craig, who has been, is, and will always be answerable to us.

Craig smiles and nods approval.

MS. DIANA   He's proven himself trustworthy, and over the course of time has stepped into the shoes of being my close confidant. Anything that concerns him concerns me, and anything that concerns me concerns him. (Beat)

You will be accountable to him for every activity involving your accomplishments for this organization. Anything he says about this organization is true. (Beat) He's not to be questioned.

Ms. Diana flashes her eyes at Maya. Ms. Diana paces.

MS. DIANA   He will assist you with anything you

need and will help you understand those areas of our activities you do not seem to understand. (Beat)
Whatever he wants from you at any time, give it to him. Otherwise, we will use our influence to invoke the long arm of the law against you.

Ms. Diana stops pacing and gazes at Maya.

MS. DIANA   With that being said, let's observe the initiation.

Ms. Diana looks at Craig with a humorless smile.

MS. DIANA   Craig, you know your job. I will be sitting on my throne watching you having fun with her, as will all of my initiates. Let's begin.

Ms. Diana sits on her throne.

MAYA (O.S.)
(Screams)

Scene 35
INT: RED ROOM – LATER – DAY
Ms. Diana sits with a satisfied smile.

MAYA (O.S.)   *(Sobs)*
Craig picks up the bucket.
Craig pours some of the liquid and passes the bucket to one of the others who does the same.
Closeup of a sobbing Maya.
An androgynous, spirit like, entity appears to disappear into Maya.
Ms. Diana stands and steps forward.
Craig and the others take Maya to Ms. Diana. Ms. Diana puts the ALC chain around her neck.

MS. DIANA   Welcome to the ALC.
Ms. Diana hugs Maya.
MS. DIANA   Now, you'll not only know who you are, but you'll know your destiny. In addition, you will live the alternative lifestyle your father denied you all these years. (Beat)
                     Please, ensure you have the creed, vision, and mission statements as contained in the manual in your memory. For this will be the motivation behind the successes of your activities for us.
Ms. Diana steps back and smiles.
MS. DIANA *(Up-beat voice)* Craig will communicate the rest of the details to you.

Scene 36
INT: BUS – NIGHT
The group boards the bus.
Craig and Maya sit next to each other. Craig hands a booklet to Maya.

CRAIG   Here is the manual. (Pause) As Ms. Diana says. "you're ripe to be a thoroughbred."
The bus moves off.

Scene 37
INT: PRINCIPAL'S OFFICE – DAY
An irate Samuel, standing, is in the principal's office.
The PRINCIPAL sits behind his desk.

SAMUEL   You tell me nobody has seen Maya! That is not possible!
PRINCIPAL   She never arrived at school that day.

	Nobody saw her that day.
SAMUEL	And that's it!
PRINCIPAL	That's not it. When you told us she didn't come home, we immediately notified the police. It's in their hands.
SAMUEL	I've been to the police many times. They don't know anything. My Maya is missing for 6 months, and they have no information of her whereabouts. What kind of a police force do we have!

Scene 38
INT: CRAIG'S APARTMENT - DAY
The window has a view of an upscale suburb. Craig sits in an easy chair as Maya lies on the couch.

MAYA	I am beginning to sense I'm on the right track to fulfill my destiny. (Beat) It's about time this young girl grew up and took her destiny into her own hands. Now I see that my dad is nothing but a liar. He has been deceiving me all this time! (Pause) I know. I'll stage a quarrel that will get him to throw me out of the house. This way, I'll gain the freedom to pursue my destiny.

Maya jumps from the couch. She paces.

MAYA	In the first place, my dad is keeping me in the dark, not telling me the truth about myself and caging me in the name of moral training.

Maya stops, faces a wall, and puts her hands on her hips.

MAYA	To be candid, I am sick and tired of your crap! If not for the ALC's influence, I'd still be in this bondage called morality!

She shakes her head wildly.

MAYA   Oh my God, I've been imprisoned! But one thing I know for sure is that my freedom has come! I'm free! Free! Following Ms. Diana's instructions, I will have to wait till my dad comes home so that I can take the fight to him. (Chuckles)
First, I'll welcome him with a couple of slaps to his cheeks. And I know he will repay me. But the results will be in my power and I will call Ms. Diana afterward!

Scene 39
INT: SAMUEL'S FRONT DOOR – NIGHT
Samuel enters and Maya slaps him in the face twice. Samuel staggers back.

SAMUEL   What the hell has come over you, Maya?
MAYA   Get lost, Dad!
SAMUEL   (Yelling) Maya, you're telling your dad to get lost? I'll teach you how to get lost instead!
Samuel pummels Maya with his fists.
Maya finds herself on the floor bleeding profusely from the head.
Maya makes a staggering run to her room.

Scene 40
INT: MAYA'S ROOM – NIGHT
Maya takes out her cell phone and makes a couple of strokes with her finger.

Scene 41

EXT: SAMUEL'S FRONT DOOR – NIGHT
Samuel has Maya by the hand as he takes her outside.
There is a police car and an ambulance, both with its lights flashing. There are a couple of other cars. Two POLICE OFFICERS grab Samuel.
Craig puts his arm around and leads her to two PARAMEDICS. Ms. Diana is with two LAWYERS.
Maya flashes Ms. Diana a smile.

SAMUEL (O.S.) This is insane!
POLICE OFFICER (O.S.) Anything you can will be used against you.

Scene 42
INT: A HOSPITAL ROOM – NIGHT
Maya, lying in bed, is the only patient in the room. Ms. Diana and her Lawyers are also the room.

MS. DIANA The next step is to make you an emancipated minor. (Beat) The longer you complain of having pains the more it will help your case. (Beat)
Granted your case is strong but as my lawyers tell me anything can happen in court so anything that will strengthen your case is to your advantage.

Scene 43
INT: OUTSIDE A COURT ROOM – DAY
Samuel is with his lawyer, TRACY BROOKS.

SAMUEL You are supposed to be the best. You never lost a case.
TRACY The best knows the situation. All evidence is on the side of the prosecution.

(Beat) A "not guilty" plea would only convince the judge you have no regret for your actions. (Beat)
The reality is you admitted to the police you beat your daughter. Your daughter ended up in the hospital.

Scene 44
INT: A COURT ROOM – DAY
Samuel and Tracy Brooks stand before the judge.

JUDGE   Having pleaded guilty to assaulting your daughter and causing here severe injury. I fine you 10,000 Rands, to be paid to your daughter. (Beat)
Maya you are an emancipated minor. You may choose a willing guardian. (Pause)
I warn you to stay away from Maya. Any repeat and the penalty won't be so lenient. (Beat) Case closed.

The judge BANGS the gavel.

Scene 45
EXT: COURT HOUSE – DAY
Maya hands the check to Ms. Diana.
Written under "For", in long hand, is "Ms. Diana's ALC for Juveniles of Broken Homes".

MS. DIANA   You see how we all help each other.

Scene 46
INT: CRAIG'S APARTMENT - DAY
A calendar on the wall shows January 2000. Maya opens an envelope. She reads the letter.

CRAIG What does it say?
MAYA I passed the Cambridge General Certificate Examination.
CRAIG Congratulations.
MAYA Thank you, not that passing means anything. I won't be attending.
CRAIG Why not?
MAYA Ms. Diana and you have taught me. The ALC will give me what I crave for in life, which is to find my destiny by living the alternative lifestyle as a juvenile. (Pause) It has the answer to who I am, really. (Beat) Strange it is but it's nothing but the truth.

Scene 47
INT: CRAIG'S APARTMENT - DAY
Craig is packing luggage bags. There is a sofa next to a coffee table.

CRAIG I'm the happiest man on earth! I have the most precious jewel living with me! (Beat) In fact, I'm your guardian angel!
Maya makes eye contact with Craig.
MAYA That's all well and good, but I would like to know what's next in the ALC's agenda.
CRAIG (Angry) If you listened carefully to what Ms. Diana said, you will remember that my word is law. I'm not to be questioned! In fact, Ms. Diana and I are not to be questioned because we are the ALC! (Beat)
I'm the representation of the ALC.

Remember, I'm your guide. All I require of you is your patience. Everything will come along fine, and you'll be able to find your destiny.

(Conciliatory) Let me go get the blueprint of what the agendas are.

Craig steps through a door with a sign the reads, "For Craig Only". Craig comes out with some papers with cryptic writing. He motions for Maya to sit on the sofa.
Maya sits and Craig sits next to her.
He puts the cryptic writing on the coffee table.
He runs his index finger through the cryptic writing.

CRAIG   All the codifications you see can be plainly state as thus. (Pause) The 39th Initiate of the ALC is a unique element that will make the assembly functional, influential, and affluent in all quarters of society. But for these feats to be attained the following must be understood and carried out. (Pause)

"A". The necessary relativistic good and evil elements known as stealing. (Pause)

"B". The opposing, yet related positives and negatives of prostitution. (Pause)

"C". Th black and white of drug trafficking.

MAYA   What do you mean?

CRAIG   (Loud voice) I will explain just hold your tongue and listen! (Normal voice)

By "the relativistic good and evil elements known as stealing", it means that the 39th Initiate must follow through on all the activities ascribed to him or her for a full year. (Beat)

During that time, he or she must savor the pleasures of the good side of his or her actions and endure the pain and pressure associated with their evil side. (Beat)

Also, "the opposing yet related positives and negatives of prostitution" involves the active participation of the 39th Initiate to savor the pleasures of positively entwining sexually with the opposite sex in addition to enduring the negative pain of the activity. (Beat)

By "the black and white of drug trafficking", it means that the initiate must observe what it takes to colorfully involve his or herself in the black of its herculean nature to enjoy the white of what it brings.

Craig gives Maya a meaningful look.

CRAIG   You are the 39th Initiate, and you're the one that will make this organization attain the heights of influence, affluence, and functionality.

MAYA   What is it, exactly, am I supposed to do? What are my activities?

CRAIG   Flip over the sacred blueprint. (Beat) There you will see what you will be doing. I will read them out for your understanding.

Maya flips the paper. Craig looks over the writing.

CRAIG   This is what you will be doing, in simple terms. (Pause) Assignment 1 (Pause) Stealing (Pause) April 30, 2000, 2 PM, the initiate will pose as someone seeking a scholarship from the gold merchant, Van Brussels. (Beat)

He awards scholarships to each and every student in all the states in the Republic of South Africa whose applications were approved two weeks after the announcement of the scholarships on radio, TV, and newspapers by his or her school. It's a once-a-year program. Students are selected from each known secondary school in every state.

Craig looks up.

CRAIG Being friends with Van Brussels, Ms. Diana was able to squeeze your name into the list, despite the fact that it's been about a year since you finished secondary school, and since she last taught there. (Beat)
This is also a vital period for Van, because his office will have just gotten a shipment of carats of gold from the mines.

Craig draws a deep breath and gives Maya a stern look.

CRAIG Now this is very important, so listen closely. You will pull a gun out of the bag you'll be carrying, and he must be shot dead.

Maya springs from the sofa.

MAYA No! I can do many things, but not that!

Craig pulls Maya onto the sofa. Maya struggles but he subdues her. He pulls Maya's face close to his.

CRAIG You want to fulfill your destiny, right? You wanted this and don't you forget it. You don't want to disappoint Ms. Diana after all that she has done for you, do you?

Craig's eyes narrow.

CRAIG And remember, we own you now.

Tears form in Maya's eyes. She nods. She gives a short sob. Craig releases Maya and gives her a curt nod.

CRAIG By the way, he is a close friend to Ms. Diana, but he doesn't really know what she's into. This information was given to me by

Ms. Diana, who got it from Henry Yale, close aide to Van Brussels. (Beat)

The security guards will be absent while you are performing your duty. Every member has been paid to be conveniently elsewhere, courtesy of her influence through Henry Yale. (Beat)

No one will take notice of you, provided you leave no trace.

Craig runs his index finger down the paper.

CRAIG Assignment 2 (Pause) Prostitution (Pause) July 18, 2000: Pimp X will need your services during a political function involving service chiefs in Harare, Zimbabwe. (Beat)

All of your expenses, including air fare, meals, and hotel expenses will be provided for. At this point, all you need to be aware of is that you will leave for Harare and Ms. Diana will link you up with Ninja X, his close guard, who will take you to Pimp X. (Pause)

August 15, 2000: Big Daddy from Maseru, Lesotho, needs you to be his girl for one night. This is a little more tasking, because you will face competition from other ladies who will be brought in from neighboring countries. (Beat)

You have to ensure that you carry along with you, condoms that would ensure some protection. Big Daddy is a careless sex addict who can afford anything found under a woman's skirt. (Beat)

The ALC, through Ms. Diana, would instruct you on what to do about this so that you will

have a lead over the others. (Pause)
September 12, 2000: The Real Don and his colleagues need your marathon sex service for a night in Gaborone, Botswana. Yes, on this assignment you will have to use the extra-sensory perception training you went through. (Beat)
The people you are about to deal with are killers, and are involved in many vices. The use of your extra-sensory perception would come in handy.

Maya appears nervous and physically uncomfortable.

CRAIG   October 3, 2000: The prince in Swaziland needs your company for a week. Although he doesn't really know who you are, I sense that Ms. Diana must have told him some things about you that got him interested. (Beat)
But she would have to call him directly herself, because the security is so tight that anyone who would have access to the prince must be friends to him. (Beat)
This must be two days before the D-Day itself. (Pause)
December 8, 2000: The Big Man, a media top-notch in Cape Town, South Africa, will need you for two days. Interestingly, Ms. Diana told me that they both attended the same elementary school, back in the day. (Beat)
In my opinion, gaining access to The Big Man will be the easiest. Though I've only met him once, he appears to be a nice person. By the time you meet him, you'll sure

appreciate his company!
Craig scans the paper.
CRAIG   How Ms. Diana worked those schedules out is none of my business. (Frowns) But I do know that my business is to tell you what to do, as instructed!
Craig looks at the paper.
CRAIG   Assignment 3. (Pause) Drug Trafficking. (Pause) Courier to Nelspruit Axis – February 3, 2001. (Beat)
Courier to Bloemfontein area – March 21, 2001. (Beat)
Courier to Polokwane zone – April 8, 2001. (Beat)
Courier to Johannesburg perimeter – May 30, 2001. (Pause)
Here, we'll give you the direct contact details to whom and to where you'll deliver the consignments. We'll have to put you through subsequent extra-sensory, martial-arts-empowered, and meta-physical exercises of eternal life-force energies to empower you for the projects ahead. (Beat)
After that, the rest of the members will be supporting you with their combined physical powers, which they have been trained to use. (Beat)
However, I don't think that will be necessary, because the founder himself, from what Ms. Diana has told me, had long laid the mystical foundation for a time such as this.
MAYA   Please explain what you mean by "mystical".

Craig shrugs.
CRAIG All I can say about the mystical is that the vibratory thought patterns, which Ms. Diana has judiciously used to her advantage, deals with telepathic decoding of esoteric energy fields brough about by the elementary interaction with the male-female entity, the mystical god of the ALC, only to be fully manifested when the 39th Initiate, which is you, comes on board. (Beat) That's all I really know. (Pause)
In line with our beliefs, which are in agreement with the practices, we, the ALC, must ensure that we do all we can to vest this power upon you, because you're the bedrock of all of our would-be successes, the fulfillment of Dr. Steven's blueprint of events which the 39th Initiate, you, must do. (Beat)
In this way, we will become the most recognized juvenile confraternity in the whole of Africa, and possibly the world. We will be training you on how to combine mystic and physical power to your advantage. (Beat)
By virtue of your 39th identity in this organization, you're the only one qualified to use the powers. This success is all we need to push the ALC to its expected heights. (Beat)
That's why we're giving you the very best of true education.
Craig turns to Maya. There is a long PAUSE. Craig smiles.
CRAIG I know this is confusing to you, but in

the course of time, you'll understand everything better, by and by. This is just January 8; we still have lots of time on our side!

Maya beams with excitement.
She gives Craig an approving nod. Craig grins.

CRAIG I think you understand now.

Maya gestures for Craig to continue.

CRAIG Meeting period: Twice a month, the first and last week, at the La Pierre Hotel, the initiation ground. (Pause)
However, you'll have to go every week because of the training you're about to receive.

Maya nods joyful acceptance.

CRAIG Sharing formula. (Pause) One. Ten percent of the proceeds will go to the informants: The ALC's networks are connected to the various quarters where you will go to ply these trades. (Beat)
The informants themselves are not only linked with Ms. Diana, but they are the ones who communicate with her, to let her know when and where she should use you for various activities. (Beat)
The drug routes, pimp hang-outs, and stealing channels have our networks, and are in constant communication with us. Therefore, whatever is made from the proceeds, a tenth goes to them. (Pause)
Two. Twenty percent of the proceeds go to the force men and women through their respective service chiefs. At the helm of affairs are those who are next in command

to their bosses. (Beat)

Though Ms. Diana is connected to them all, our informants need to work closely with the service chiefs so that events will turn out in our favor. (Pause)

Three. Ten percent of the proceeds go to me: Being the pivot of this organization and by the powers vested upon Ms. Diana, I have been made not only your superior but also deserve a tithe from the sweat of your brow. (Pause)

Four. Forty percent of the proceeds go to the ALC. For the day-to-day running of the ALC, there must be enough finances to fill in the gap for any unforeseen realities in the present or future. (Pause)

Five. Fifteen percent of the proceeds go to you: "A laborer", the Bible says, "deserves his wages". The ALC is pleased to give you fifteen percent of the money because of the strength of effort you'll put in to get the assignments done. (Pause)

Six. Five percent of the proceeds go to the other initiates. The ALC rewards loyalty. Hence, to all our loyal initiates, we will give to them five percent to be shared amongst all 38 of them. (Pause)

You see, the arrangements of the dates were mysteriously orchestrated by the founder, the late Dr. Steven, at a period when important events will be taking place. (Beat) This is a mystery only you can make simple and plain to all of us. Ms. Diana is just working according to the set plan. It's just

that there are some powers working for her.
Craig hands the paper to Maya. Craig stands, stretches, and YAWNS.

CRAIG Well, enough of all that. From here on, you'll have to concentrate on the manual, meditate on it on a day-in-and-day-out basis and see what happens to you. (Beat) I know for sure you will eventually find your destiny!

MAYA I never knew you were such a genius! Yet, you pretended as though you were nothing back in school!

CRAIG Well, I'd say it's more a steadfast dedication to the cause. Like what it says in the Holy Bible, "give unto Caesar what's Caesar's and to God what's God's". (Beat) I've successfully given my now Alma Mata what they wanted from me, though at an average rating compared to yours. Hence, what you've seen so far!

Craig chuckles. He bends down and strokes Maya's face gently.

CRAIG (Whispers) The day is ebbing away. Let's spend quality time together in the other room!

Maya smiles and she walks with Craig to their room.

MONTAGE
Maya enters a room.
Ms. Diana is sitting in an armchair. Maya points at a closet.
Ms. Diana nods and presses a button.
Maya opens the closet door and takes out a bomb. Maya is on a mat in a gym.

She successfully defeats 3 opponents. Craig nods approval.
Maya sits at a small table.
Ms. Diana sits on the other side of the table. On the table there are 4 blank cards.
Maya closes her eyes.
She opens her eyes and points to each card and moves her lips.
Ms. Diana turns over each card.
The cards are a square, squiggly lines, circle, and a star. Ms. Diana smiles approval.
Maya watches a TV screen that shows Ms. Diana form a yoga pose.
Maya makes the pose.
Ms. Diana types on a keyboard and the TV screen shows Maya's pose and an outline of the correct pose.
END MONTAGE

Scene 48
INT: ROOM WITH TV - DAY
Maya is watching a large television screen. Ms. Diana presses a remote.

ON SCREEN
Maya enters a luxurious office where Van Brussels is sitting on a sofa. There are bars of gold on a table.
Van Brussels beacons Maya to come and sit by the desk. Maya walks to the chair. She reaches into a handbag and takes out a handgun, aims it at Van Brussels' head and fires two rounds. Van Brussels collapses.
Maya puts the gun in the bag. She sweeps the bars of gold into her bag. She casually exits the room.

OFF SCREEN
MS. DIANA   Mission made easy.

Ms. Diana hands the remote to Maya.
MS. DIANA   Replay this, many times. Focus on every detail. This is what you will see and this is how you will act.
Ms. Diana steps out of the room.

Scene 49
EXT: A MANSION – DAY
It is surrounded by trees and natural landscaping. Maya approaches the front door.

Scene 50
INT: LIVING ROOM - DAY
Van Brussels sits on a sofa. Henry Yale enters.

HENRY   The next student goes by the name Maya Isaacs. She is in her final year at the Steven Beak Comprehensive Secondary School, and a student of Ms. Diana, your good friend.
VAN BRUSSELS   Let her come in. (Beat) She is the last on the list of scholarship awardees.
Van Brussels rubs his eyes.
VAN BRUSSELS   It's not easy attending to over 300 students across the states for scholarship purposes.
Henry Yale nods understanding.
VAN BRUSSELS   I've known Ms. Diana for years, but I haven't seen her for a long time. However, I know that she has a good reputation for education. (Beat)
Her students are indeed tested and trusted in their academics. So, for her choice of candidate to be Maya, then she is worth

being given a scholarship award.
Van Brussels looks in a folder.
VAN BRUSSELS   Interestingly, it's like saving the best for the last. I'm going to be adding Maya to my list. The candidate chosen by one of my best friends!
Van Brussels waves his hand.
VAN BRUSSELS   Bring her in, and then you can go, Henry, I will be with you later.

Scene 51
EXT: A MANSION - DAY
Henry exits from the front door.

Scene 52
INT: LIVING ROOM - DAY
Maya enters.

VAN BRUSSELS   Welcome. Take seat.
Van Brussels points to the seat near the sofa. Van Brussels stands.
VAN BRUSSELS   I'm a little bit uncomfortable right now. (Beat) I've been attending to over 100 students for the past 2 hours. Please, let me take some seconds to pace back and forth. I need some exercise. Hope you don't mind?
MAYA   No problem sir!
Maya places her hand in the bag. Van Brussels steps out of the room.
MAYA   (Whispering) Pull a gun out of the bag you'll be carrying, and he must be shot dead.
Van Brussels enters and sits on the sofa. Maya pulls out the handgun and points it a Van Brussels' head.

MAYA On your knees, Van Brussels, with your hands up in the air! Close your eyes. And if you think what I'm holding is a toy, you will leave me with no choice but to put some bullets into you! (Beat)
All I need are the bars of gold and one other thing. (Beat) I will let you know.
Van Brussels falls to his knees.
VAN BRUSSELS What are you up to, Maya? I thought you were Ms. Diana's best candidate. I've known her as someone who sends the best, and that's not what I'm seeing right now! (Pause) I don't want to believe she sent you to me! This was not what I was told about you. Who are you, Maya? What do you want, young woman? (Beat)
Please, just drop your gun. I will give you more than what you want, far better than the scholarship package.
Van Brussels is sweating and unsteady.
MAYA You are too young for what you are about to do! You can have the gold.
He moves to point to the gold. Maya pushes the gun closer to his head. Van Brussels motions towards the bars with his head.
VAN BRUSSELS That's it on the table. But don't kill me! You are too precious to be wasted. I believe in you. I know you were compelled by men and women of the underworld to do what you don't want to do. (Beat)
You are a great woman! You are a young woman with great potential. Don't do what you're about to do!
Tears form in Maya's eyes.

MAYA (Curt tone) I'm sorry, but I have been mandated to do what I have to do. I'd have loved to help you out if I had my way! I'm sorry, this is what I was told to do with you! Releasing the bullets into your body is the very thing I also require. Goodnight Van!

Maya shoots Van Brussels twice in the head. Van Brussels falls dead. Maya puts the gun in the bag. She sweeps the bars of gold into her bag.

Scene 53
EXT: A MANSION - DAY
Maya exits the front door. She walks at a quick pace.

Scene 54
EXT: CRAIG'S APARTMENT - DAY
Maya steps out of a cab and walks at a quick pace towards the apartment.

MONTAGE:
Maya is taken to a backroom of a night club.
It's a smoke-filled room with gaudy, albeit expensive, furnishings.
There is a man seated in a large armchair.
Maya is led into the back of a stretch limousine.
She sits next to a man who is wearing a lot of expensive jewelry.
Maya, in a formal gown, is ushered through a room filled with people in formal dress.
She is taken to a heavily bemedaled man in a flamboyant military uniform.
Maya shown into a large room. The room has many trophies on the walls. At the far end of the room there is a man in a papasan chair.

END MONTAGE:

Scene 55
INT: RED ROOM – DAY
Maya sits at a table across from Ms. Diana.

MS. DIANA All hands must be on desk, so to speak, as we attain the full potential of our goal. (Beat)
To be the most respected teen confraternity in Africa and possibly the world. (Pause)
First and foremost, Maya, you will have to employ every caution here. Just as you've done in the past, you must use all of the combined effects of the physical and mystical powers you've been taught. (Beat)
What I'm trying to say is, don't let your past successes get into your head and make you careless! (Pause)
I have done my part. Contacts are being made throughout the destination perimeters you will go to deliver the parcels in your possession. (Beat)
But your part will have to be played to ensure the success we aspire to, using you as the 39th Initiate. As the courier, you will have to take the following steps. (Pause)
You must be in Nelspruit before February 3rd, because the drug lord, Baron Da Mafia, my good friend, has informed me, through his personal assistant, Mr. Deliverer, that there are loads of competitors around the Nelspruit axis who will be arriving with the same 50 kilos worth of narcotics. (Beat)

In his words, "If you don't come before the date, I can guarantee you, madam, you will miss him! (Pause)

This is how you'll go about it. On February 1, I will pay for your plane ticket to Nelspruit and for the Nelspruit Hotel, where you'll be lodged.(Beat)

The moment you're there, please call my number. Then I will call Mr. Deliverer, letting him know that you're in town, and he will send an agent to come pick you up at the hotel. (Beat)

You'll be at the place of Baron Da Mafia, friends with Mr. Deliverer, until the date of delivery.

Ms. Diana grins.

MS. DIANA   This will prevent other competitors from snatching this opportunity. It's almost as if the whole sale has been handed to us on a platter of gold!

Ms. Diana and Maya exchange smiles.

MS. DIANA   Ensure that you get to know of Baron Da Mafia's whereabouts the moment you're taken to his Nelspruit mansion and inform me as well. Remember to call me.

Maya gives an impatient nod.

MS. DIANA   Don't be like that. You must listen: this is very important. With the parcel in your possession, please wait for his arrival so that he can buy the parcel at the stipulated 130,000 Rands. (Pause)

Mr. Deliverer will then take you to the Nelspruit Local Airport, where you'll board the next available flight to Durban. I'll be

                    waiting for you at the airport for the money.
Ms. Diana puts a hand on Maya's shoulder.
MS. DIANA   Rest assured; all has been put together to ensure that these operations go without a hitch. All I require from you is that you do your part like you've always done. (Beat)
                    One more thing. These tactics will be the same as regards the Bloemfontein area. Polokwane zone, and Johannesburg axis drug-trade. The same rules apply, but only names that differ.
Maya has a big smile.
MAYA   Ms. Diana, be certain that this is a done deal! I can almost see my destiny now!
MS. DIANA   Maya, you're already there! Your destiny is there for you to attain!

MONTAGE:
Maya stands by as Craig packs narcotics into a luggage case.
Maya enters the Nelspruit Airport terminal wheeling the luggage case.
Craig opens a suitcase of money.
Maya stands by as Craig zips up a luggage case. An open and empty luggage case is next to it.
Maya enters the Bloemfontein Airport terminal wheeling two luggage cases.
Craig has two open suitcases of money.
Maya follows a skycap, who is wheeling a cart of luggage cases, as the skycap enters the Polokwane Airport terminal.
Craig opens a luggage case of money.
END MONTAGE:

Scene 56
INT: CRAIG'S APARTMENT - DAY
Craig is watching TV. Maya makes a halting approach to Craig.

MAYA
: Craig, something's been bothering me, and I have to ask you about it.

CRAIG
: What is it?

MAYA
: When will I get my 15 percent of the money?

CRAIG
: As soon as you're done with the whole assignment! Remember, you don't question our activities!

Scene 57
INT: CRAIG'S APARTMENT - NIGHT
Craig is agitated.

CRAIG
: I told you before! As soon as you're done with the whole assignment! I also told to before to remember; you don't question our activities!

Scene 58
INT: CRAIG'S APARTMENT - DAY
Craig is mad.

CRAIG
: You have been bothering me about this all week! For the last time! As soon as you're done with the whole assignment! For the last time! Do not question our activities!

Scene 59
INT: CRAIG'S APARTMENT - NIGHT

The only light is from the television set. Craig is sitting in a lounge chair watching television. Maya enters. She is giddy and unsteady. Craig clicks off the television set.

CRAIG   How dare you come home at this hour! This isn't the first time! You are hardly ever here! Worst of all you have failed to attend meetings as instructed! When Ms. Diana calls you to a meeting you come!

Maya walks towards the bedroom door.

MAYA   We'll talk about this in the morning.

Craig jumps from his chair.

CRAIG   We'll talk about this now!

Maya tips over a chair and dashes into the bedroom. There is the CLICK of the bedroom door lock.
Craig steps around the chair in his way.
There is the BANG of something Maya uses to barricade the bedroom door.

Scene 60
INT: CRAIG'S APARTMENT – EVENING
A stoic Maya sits at a table. Craig sits on the couch watching the TV and Maya. The TV changes to a commercial.
Craig steps out of the room. A door CLOSES. Maya steps out of the apartment and SILENTLY closes the door behind her.

Scene 61
EXT: THE STREET – EVENING
Maya hails a cab.

Scene 62
INT: CRAIG'S APARTMENT – EVENING
The living room is empty. There is the muffled sound of a FLUSHING TOILET. The bathroom door swings open.

Craig scans the living room. He opens the bedroom door. He rushes out of the apartment.

Scene 63
INT: DURBAN NIGHTCLUB – NIGHT
The music is loud, and the club is dark. Maya nurses a drink at a corner table.

MAYA
It appears I've been brainwashed. I've been following a very vague path to my so-called destiny. True self. (Beat)
Anyway, I have harbored the sleep of mistakes and it's about time I engaged my waking of corrections! But before I do that, I'll have to give Ms. Diana, Craig, and the entirely sick ALC a taste of their poison.

Maya takes a sip of her drink, and her angry expression turns to a sardonic smile.

MAYA
This next assignment is going to be different. I'm going to do things my own way! This time around, the proceeds from the deal are all mine! (Beat)
I don't care, and I damn the whole consequences of what might happen between me and the ALC. After all, I have my connections in the whole of Johannesburg, and I trust my connection, Carr Singles, to do the job for me! (Beat)
When I get the money from him at D'People Pub in Johannesburg, I'll be on my way out of South Africa to Paris to enjoy myself. All I need do is to ensure that the money is paid to me, not to Ms. Diana again! (Beat)
May 30, 2001 mustn't pass me by!

Scene 64
EXT: A DURAN SIDE STREET – DAY
Maya is along on the street. Maya punches numbers into a cell phone.

CARR SINGLES (O.C.) Hello.
MAYA This is Maya. I need for you to do a job for me.
CARR SINGLES (O.C.) What is the job?
MAYA No questions asked.
CARR SINGLES (O.C.) How can I do a job if I don't know what it is?
MAYA After our meeting at the pub I need for you to call Ms. Diana an tell her you were stuck in traffic and be late for our meeting.
CARR SINGLES (O.C.) You want me to report I will be late for the meeting after I attended the meeting?
MAYA Exactly.
CARR SINGLES (O.C.) Any I should do this for nothing?
MAYA I'll make it worth your while.
CARR SINGLES (O.C.) Call me again in 30 minutes and we'll see if what you think is worth my while is what I consider worth my while.
MAYA I'll talk to you in 30 minutes.

Maya powers off the phone. She walks to a trash receptacle. She scans the area. She tosses the phone in the receptacle.

Scene 65
INT: MS. DIANA'S OFFICE – DAY
Ms. Diana is alone in her luxurious office. A cell phone rings. Ms. Diana opens the phone and checks the number.

MS. DIANA   What is it?
CARR SINGLES (O.C.)   I just got a call from the person I'm supposed to meet.
MS. DIANA   I'm sorry there was no reason to call you.
CARR SINGLES (O.C.)   That's what I thought. I was asked to call to tell you I'd be late for the meeting after the meeting was over.
MS. DIANA   You were told to report you would be late for a meeting you already attended?
CARR SINGLES (O.C.)   That's correct. I'm supposed to get a call in about 20 minutes to discuss the price. (Beat) Please advise.
MS. DIANA   Ask for twice the opening bit than accept the counter bid. (Beat) I'll call you if I need anything else. (Beat) Thank you for keeping me in the loop.

Ms. Diana closes her phone.

Scene 66
EXT: MS. DIANA'S LODGE – DAY
It's a large porch with expensive furnishings.
Craig and Ms. Diana are sitting on lounge chairs sipping whisky.

MS. DIANA   Craig, I'm very surprised about Maya's behavior. She thinks she can take us for a ride. Who does she think she is?
CRAIG   Please, what do you mean, Ms. Diana?
MS. DIANA   Craig, do you know that Maya wants to put us out of the Johannesburg drug deal?
CRAIG   What do you mean? This can't be possible! Maya is the most trusted initiate

we have. She knows the implications of violating the rules of the ALC! Who told you this?

MS. DIANA My dear Craig, Carr Singles did. Remember that for every assignment Maya has covered, the ALC has had informants who were planted to monitor her moves and report back to me.

CRAIG Going by what you've said, that means the mystical power is about to dim in its illuminating power of greatness.

An agitated Craig stands and paces.

CRAIG Ms. Diana, what do we do now? It appears that Maya has suddenly de-programmed herself from our spell! I see danger coming!

MS. DIANA Where is your faith, Craig?

She takes a sip of whisky.

MS. DIANA It appears you've been carried away by what has happened.

She smiles, leans forward and gestures for Craig to sit.

MS. DIANA All we need do is to put Maya behind bars.

She frowns.

MS. DIANA But by doing so, all my phone lines, would have to be disposed of and put out of the GPS coverage areas in this country.

She waves and sighs.

MS. DIANA For sure, we'll get a replacement for Maya in time. But she must be seriously punished.

CRAIG I agree with you. Maya deserves to be revealed to the law-loving general public! We have to deal with her now!

MS. DIANA   I'm grateful to Carr Singles for this information. I have known him for years as one who can be relied on when it comes to information. (Beat) Provided the money is there to be paid.

She makes fists.

MS. DIANA   For without him, Maya would have gotten away with the life-changing 100 Million Rand deal!

CRAIG   I'd have found out sooner or later.

Ms. Diana gives Craig a cold look.

MS. DIANA   Don't forget that Carr is part of the Johannesburg police team, working for the ALC as an informant. This is why I trusted him to tell me the truth. (Beat)
Now we'll have to use our connections in the police force and have Carr work for us, pretending to be working with her as her connection. (Beat)
Then he will secretly engage the service of the Johannesburg police to come arrest her!

CRAIG   You're indeed a goddess, but the physical type! You have everything all planned out from inception! It's really good to be associate with a goddess!

MS. DIANA   Don't flatter me, Craig. I know what I'm called for, and I'm here to protect the faith at all costs. That is all.

Ms. Diana grabs a calendar.

MS. DIANA   Now, today's date is-
CRAIG   May 27, 2001.
MS. DIANA   Yes! I will put a call through to Carr Singles about what we've discussed. After that, we will disengage our phone lines.

CRAIG	Okay, Ms. Diana.

Scene 67
INT: D'PEOPLE PUB – DAY
Maya waits in a corner booth. CARR SINGLES sits at the booth.

MAYA	I have the consignment. I have it at the hotel.
CARR	Which hotel.
MAYA	The one just a few buildings away. (Pause) If you will follow me, you can have your consignment. Do you have the money as we agreed, Carr?
CARR	Yes, Maya. Don't you trust me? Let's go to the hotel, since you said that is where the consignment is. Remember, all I need do is to call my boss. (Beat)
	You know, Mr. Bruce, about the consignment, and you know what happens. Your check will be signed right away. It's that simple. Maya, let's go to the hotel and see what you got.

Scene 68
INT: CAR – DAY
Two uniformed officers are in this unmarked car across the street from the pub.
A man in civilian clothes nods to them. Carr Singles and Maya leave the Pub.
A man in civilian clothes makes an indistinct gesture.
The officer in the passenger seat picks up the radio transmitter.

Scene 69
INT: HOTEL CORRIDOR - DAY
Maya and Carr Singles walk to a hotel room door. Maya unlocks the door. There are INDISTINCT VOICES and RUNNING FEET. Maya turns and sees JEN ROBINS, and other plain clothes officers.

JEN   Johannesburg police! Put your hands above your heads! You have the right to remain silent. Anything you say will be used against you in a court of law!
Lady, open the door. Let's see what's in the room.
Police Officer Robins shows Maya a search warrant.
MAYA   Let me call my lawyer, please.

Scene 70
INT: HOTEL ROOM - DAY
Maya sits on the bed. Plain clothes and uniformed officers mill around the room. One officer takes a bag of a white substance. Another officer tests the contents and nods.

JEN   Woman, I don't think that will be necessary!
Turns to JAKE.
JEN   Jake, handcuff her.
Jake handcuffs Maya. Three uniformed officers take her towards the door.
JEN   It's a pleasure working with you, Singles. You're an asset to the force. Well done!
Jen Robins pats Carr Singles on his back.
MAYA   You set me up! Carr, why did you do this to me? I can't believe you betrayed me at

	a time I needed you the most! I didn't know that you have been my enemy all this time! (Beat) I've made the biggest mistake of my life, trusting you, Carr! I never knew you were a policeman! You bastard!
CARR	Never trust anyone, Maya! (Beat) Never bite the fingers that fed you! Never bite the hands of Ms. Diana! You can rant all you like, but the long arm of the law has caught up with you. (Beat) Good riddance to bad rubbish!

Scene 71
INT: JOHANNESBURG COURT ROOM – DAY
Maya stands with her lawyer. The JUDGE sits at the bench.

JUDGE	Maya Isaacs having pleaded guilty to possession with intent to sell 30 kilos of narcotics I sentence you to 3 years confinement. (Beat) Case Closed.

The Judge bangs the gavel.

Scene 72
INT: JAIL CELL – DAY
There are 4 bunk beds and a ceiling fan. MAMA, KHADIJAH, and MERCY are the inmates.
A JAILER opens the cell gate and Maya, bed linens in hand, steps in. The jailer closes and locks the gate behind Maya.

Scene 73
INT: JAIL CELL – DAY
Maya is fighting with Mercy.
Mama steps between them and pushes them back.

Scene 74
INT: JAIL CELL – DAY
Maya is fighting with Khadijah. Maya takes Khadijah to the floor. Mama pulls Maya off Khadijah and flings Maya across the cell.

MAMA Togetherness is all that counts! For the past 3 weeks, we've been trying to reason with you, and to get along with you. You aren't considerate. (Beat)
Respect is reciprocal you know. We have similar reasons why we are in this prison. But one thing is sure. The 4 of us are not just here by coincidence. (Beat)
I believe there is something we will all learn from each other that will change the remaining parts of our lives. Young woman, for your good, learn to behave the way we behave. (Beat)
I'm sure that you've seen for the past 3 weeks how organized and united the 3 of us are. The jailer had no cause to come in to settle any rift among us. (Beat)
What has kept us safe and out of trouble since the beginning of our stay in prison is the order we follow. However, ever since you came into prison, we have been having heated arguments, arguing with you, even giving some of us cause to beat you up.
(Beat) The jailer has had to come and lecture us, which has never happened before. For your sake and for the general peace of everyone, I want you to behave yourself. (Beat)

Follow our character rules, or else your experience will be bitter, of that I can assure you. You'll like our company better if you do what we do.

Khadijah and Mercy, sitting on their beds, nod agreement

Scene 75
INT: JAIL CELL - LATER - DAY
The women sit on their beds and share an occasional glance. Maya drops to her knees.

MAYA I'm sorry for what I have caused you all. I promise it won't happen again. I'm willing to cooperate with you guys, no matter what. (Beat)
To be truthful, I'm tired of doing things on my own while seeing you do your things together. I know I have acted stupid all this time.

Tears form in Maya's eyes.

MAYA Please, see me as your baby sister!

The other inmates go to Maya.

MAMA From the moment the jailer opened the prison door to have you going us, I sensed a graced woman who is here, not only to serve her prison sentence, but learn from the School of Hard Knocks what it means to live a grace filled life. (Beat)
By and by, you will understand what I am telling you. (Pause) Unfortunately, your childish attitude hasn't helped matters since you came here. But now that you've seen your wrongs, we will help to give your stay in prison something positive to

                    remember. (Beat)
                    My intuition strongly tells me that you'll be released before the stipulated prison sentence is up. So, while you're with us, let's get to know each other better; nationality, background, why we are here, and other things. (Beat)
                    With this knowledge, I believe, we will begin to learn things that will help us understand why we are here.
MERCY   Please get up. (Beat) If she could forgive you, then so can we.

Khadijah nods agreement.

MAYA   Whatever you day is what I will follow. I really want to learn what I ought to have learned. I promise you will always listen to what you have to tell me.

Scene 76
INT: JAIL CELL – NIGHT
Maya sits on a lower bunk next to Mama. Mercy and Khadijah sit on the opposite lower bunk.

MAMA   I will start the ball rolling. Our stories will be told in this format. It will begin with me, followed by Fatimah, then Mercy, and finally you, Maya. (Beat)
                    I decided to make it this way based on the number of years each inmate has spent here. With that being said, it's time for me to get started. (Pause)
                    I go by the name Adanna Jenifer Ezekwe. I am the second child but the first daughter of a family of 7; 3 boys and 4 girls. My father

died when I was 7 years old. (Beat)

My elder brother, David Ezekwe, had died earlier, before my father, under mysterious circumstances. Mother had to endure every sacrifice imaginable to give us the best of education, clothing, and training so that we could be like the children in the village. (Beat)

I hail from Umueche village in Abia North of Abia State, Nigeria. Life was a living hell as we grew older because of the incessant increase in the cost of living. (Beat)

As a result, Mother looked forward to the time when I would be hired as a housemaid in the city. (Pause)

Mother's dream came true when one of her distant relatives came all the way from Lagos to the village to visit her rarely- seen extended family members. (Beat)

Fortunately, she was able to see that Mother could not afford the expense of raising 6 children. Madam Ify, as she was fondly called, promised to take me down to Lagos. (Beat)

To show how serious she was, Madam Ify gave Mother a sum of 15,000 Naira. That was a huge sum of money at that time. This was in 1992. (Beat)

Madam Ify promised she would return to the village in the next 2 weeks to take me along to Lagos, since she did not come prepared to see me in the first place. (Pause)

As a child, I had always dreamt of living in the city, supporting my mother with the proceeds I made and helping to train my younger siblings, since it was the tradition of the Ibo tribe for the first child to assume responsibility of taking care of other members of his or her immediate family. (Beat)

During Madam Ify's stay in the village, she told us how exciting a place Lagos was; the great buildings, the good roads, and the comfortable lifestyle of the people. (Beat)

She claimed that she was living in the elite area of Victoria Island and worked as a supervising officer at the National Ports Authority in Lagos. (Beat)

I looked forward to the day when I would be with her in Lagos and working in that company. No matter the peanuts I received, it was no matter, provided my people would get to eat from the profits of my sweat. (Pause)

In exactly 2 weeks, Madam Ify was back in the village, fully ready to take me along with her to Lagos. Seeing the level of my preparedness, she gave Mother a sum of 25,000 Naira and foodstuffs: tubers of yam, 2 bags of rice and beans, large bottles of groundnut oil, tins of tomatoes and packages of onions, bags of salt and sugar, and some other things for my siblings. (Beat)

Mother showed great appreciation for her gesture. She would not have to labor again as her dream came to pass. Mother was able to set up her small trade business at the village square. (Beat)

At that moment I knew the living condition of Mother and my siblings would improve immensely. (Pause)
But this came at a price unknown to them: me. Mother cried when she saw me leave her and her other children, and head out of the house along with Madam Ify to the car that would take us to Lagos. (Beat)
I think she hired the driver to do the job. I had no idea that I had been bought at a very cheap price! (Pause)
We eventually made it to Lagos after a long journey. Rather than take us to Victoria Island, where she claimed she was residing, she took us to the home of one of her friends and instructed me to get out of the car with my bag. (Beat)
Then the driver drove off to God knows where! (Pause)
I was beginning to realize the troubles I would be in for. In her small apartment, I slept through the night in the company of heat and many house flies. (Beat)
One week later, I was feeling seriously sick, but because of how strong my body was, I recovered and continued to accept what she had to offer. (Pause)
Two months after we arrived there, Madam Ify introduced me into the business of hawking. I hawked bottled water and canned soft and alcoholic drinks. (Beat)
She ensured that I sold all she gave me for the day to sell by threatening that, if I didn't, she would not give me dinner. I used to leave

home as early as 6:30 AM to hit the streets of Oshodi to hawk, and get home as late as 8:30 PM, with everything completely sold. (Beat)
This was happening towards the later part of 1992. I was 15 years old. (Pause)
Meanwhile, Madam Ify was fond of telling my mother that all was well, when in reality, I was going through hell on earth! (Beat)
As fate would have it, one Saturday morning, I bumped into one of our big brothers, a cousin really, who was surprised to see me looking tattered, and hawking along that busy road. (Beat)
I told him all that was happening to me and what I was going through at the hands of madam Ify. He promised he would take the matter to the village. He was never seen again. (Pause)
One time, I came home after work very terrified. I didn't make any good sales for the day. She beat the living daylights out of me. (Beat)
When I couldn't take it any longer, I ran away from the house and started living under the Oshodi Bridge. I was there for two weeks. (Beat)
Madam Ify didn't bother looking for me. When I couldn't bear the harsh realities of living outside, I went back to her, pleading for her to take me back; that I would do anything without any complaints. (Beat)
She told me she hadn't worried about me because she knew I would find my way back to her place. (Pause)

Surprisingly, Madam Ify took me away from hawking. She told me she wanted to introduce me to a better business. For 2 weeks, I just ate, slept, and watched television. (Beat)

As a naïve teenage girl, I thought all was becoming well. I had no idea that more problems were on their way! (Pause)

Three weeks later, we left Lagos for Benin City, Edo state, Nigeria. There, we were living in a more spacious 3-bedroom flat. All seemed rosy, but one thing got me wondering: what was this woman really up to when different men came to have whispered discussions with her in the house, while staring at me during and after conversations? (Beat)

In time, I realized that I was in fact the center of their discussions! (Pause)

Madam Ify took me to a place where I met a man whose name was Charles Oba. She said to me that I would be living with him for a long time. (Beat)

She promised I would be given far better treatment if I lived with him. Traveling to countries like England, Canada, South Africa, Japan, and other countries would be all I'd be doing. (Beat)

Madam Ify promised that she would be sending my mother and siblings the money she would make by trading me. I was confused because I had no idea what she really meant. (Beat)

She left me at his mercy, not knowing how

deeply I would be soaked in the trade which was about to draw me. (Pause)

Charles Oba eventually became my agent. And at the age of 15, I lost my virginity to him. He subsequently took me to a native fetish priest, popularly known as Baba Lawo, in his village. (Beat)

There I was forced to drink a bottle of blood as a sign of allegiance. Meaning that no matter what I did or what he or the client did to me I would not divulge anything. (Beat)

Otherwise, I would die miserably and mysteriously. He commanded me to undress and placed all kinds of incisions on my body; eyes, breasts, butt, and my private part. (Beat)

The priest assured Charles that with these marks on my body, I would attract many rich male customers. He forced me to place some charms round my waist so that there would not be any attacks from enemies on me, from either the physical or the spiritual world. (Beat)

With Charles Oba carefully keeping close watch, the journey into the real world of prostitution began for me.

(Pause) He assigned me to various top government officials in the country in various strategic places, such as Abuja, Port- Harcourt, and Lagos. (Beat)

The money was pocketed by my agent and Madam Ify. To make this live livable at all, I hoped she was giving the people in my village the money. (Beat)

Whether she did it or not is, till this day, uncertain to me. (Pause) We traveled to various countries for pimping. I had the opportunity of visiting countries like Italy, where I stayed 6 months; Canada, 3 months; Germany, 2 months; the U.S., a month; and the United Arab Emirates, 4 months. (Beat)
For the first time, I was paid money directly. This meant that Madam Ify's share would be reduced by 50 percent. I started supporting my siblings thereafter for the next 5 years. (Pause)
I thought all was going well for me until Mr. Oba introduced me to a client in South Africa. His name was Isa Pierre, a diplomat in Johannesburg, South Africa. (Beat)
He took me to his hotel suite. Thinking it was a normal assignment. I was surprised for the first time in this life of mine. (Beat)
He wanted me to have sex with his two dogs for $20,000! I rejected it!
(Pause)
As he tried to force me into the act, I smashed an empty vodka bottle on his head in self-defense. As I was running out of the hotel room, people around me saw the blood on my hands. (Beat)
The hotel clerk rang the police station close by and told them that something had happened and gave my description. Then, when the housekeeper told him what he'd seen, the diplomat lying in a pool of blood, he called the Emergency Medical Team. (Pause)

Before I could board a taxi to the airport to catch the next available flight from Johannesburg, South Africa to Lagos, Nigeria, the police caught up with me. (Beat) Because of the diplomat's influence, I was arrested and charged with attempted murder and human trafficking. All I had on me, even the charms around me waist, were seized. (Beat)

I was subsequently given a prison sentence of 10 years. (Pause) My connections abandoned me. I have no idea where Madam Ify fled to. Charles Oba was never seen again. I have been on my own since the time of my arrest in 1998. (Beat)

Only my family in the village communicates with me. They send me letters saying how much they miss me and they are praying and pressing hard for my release from this prison. (Beat)

I am happy they are doing well in the village. Now that I am in prison here, I know why they say "there is nothing like family." (Pause) As I tell you this story, I have 7 years to go!

MAYA Look ahead at the beam of hope. This was a horrible thing that happened, but it's not forever. (Pause) What a story!

KHADIJAH What a horrific thing to have happen to you! I had no idea.

Tears are in Mercy's eyes.

MERCY I'm moved by your story!

MAMA Khadijah let's hear your story. You are next.

KHADIJAH   I know my ordeal in not as long as Mama's. But my story is one about the consequence of going beyond the bounds set by your parents. (Beat)
I was born a Muslim, and raised as one all my life. I have been taught by my parents to live with the strict dictates of the Holy Koran. (Beat)
I was Dad's girl all my life, but had always wished that I could enjoy life to the fullest. At the age of 13, I started mingling with people who my father and mother regarded as unclean. (Beat)
To me, I reasoned that they were people who were just being liberal with life. But to my parents, they were not to be associated with at all. (Beat)
In Alexandria, I grew up as the only child of a Jewish-Libyan mother and Egyptian father. At one time a sailor, Dad retired to take on the responsibility of being one of the leading Muslim clerics in the whole of Egypt. (Beat)
People looked up to us as role models. But I didn't like that lifestyle. (Pause)
When I was 18, a family friend talked me into schooling in South Africa. He got me a brochure of the lists of South African universities. (Beat)
As I looked at it, I admired the lifestyle of the people living in Johannesburg. What really attracted me to schooling in Johannesburg were the people, social joints, and quality of

social life. (Beat)

I convinced my dad that studying at the University of Johannesburg would be great for me. My dad, Midol Hassan, agreed to send me abroad to South Africa. (Beat)

He owns a publishing firm in Polokwane, EL-Amin Book Publishing. Preparations were made, and I though freedom had become mine. (Beat)

When the time came, I left for South Africa for the 1998/1999 academic session. (Pause) It was in my second year that I met one dashing young man in the person of Clark James, a second-year student of Industrial Chemistry. (Beat)

He was the only true love I ever knew. Clark made me the woman I am today. He promised me he would not cheat on me and would arrange to meet my parents within the next 2 years. (Beat)

Everything was going on well between us. We had fun all the time, and visited some of the more esoteric places in Cape Town, such as Pretoria and Mandela's Ounu village. (Pause)

On 1st of September, 1999, I was out doing errands, getting ready to travel home after the end of my first year. When I got back to the hostel, I saw the greatest surprise of my life; I caught Clark in the act, on the bed with my best friend? (Beat)

I took justice into my own hands by stabbing Clark to death. And before I could realize what had come over me, I discovered that

Michelle, me ex-best friend, had gone to alert everybody in the hostel about what had happened. (Beat)

It was then I knew I had committed murder! The new got to my parents, and they took it hard. They wrote to me, telling me that they've disowned me as their only child. (Beat)

But they will do the best they can to get me release from prison. As you can see, girls, that had been my plight!

Khadijah scans the others.

MAMA You never told us this before. Why didn't you tell us of this burden?

KHADIJAH Such is life! IF you didn't know, ladies, now you all know!

MERCY Mercy Laurent is my name. I was raised on the streets of Limbe, Douala, and Yaoundé in Cameroon, never knowing who my parents were. (Beat)

At the age of 6, I was molested by a man who I called my uncle. When he saw that I was about to tell his mistress, he drove me out of his house. (Beat)

All my life, the street has always been my home. I was able to speak English quite fluently because of my association with Nigerians over there. (Beat)

Drinking, smoking, clubbing, gambling, partying, and fighting were the street attitudes I carried with me wherever I went. (Pause)

At age 12, I got involved in child prostitution in Limbe. The youngest off all clients that used my services was a young man of 17 years. (Beat)

I was so used to this that I engaged in multiple-sexual relations with various male clients for money. As I grew older, my fame was spread throughout the whole area. (Beat)

Knowing that I was becoming more popular amongst some politicians, my price rose as far as $30 per round. I moved to Doula and attracted a great number of clients, especially foreigners. (Beat)

Eventually I settled in Yaoundé. There I was into politicians, businessmen, and merchants because my charges were high for professional reasons. (Pause)

A certain businessman, named Michel Foe, expressed his interest in me. I was in Yaoundé at the time. He wanted us to go to France, where I could become more educated and help grow his business. (Beat)

Michel knew I was a jump-around with guys, but he cared for me like no man had ever done. We got to France and settled first in Bordeaux, then in Nantes and finally, Paris. (Beat)

A certain middle-aged lady named Marie, who claimed to be French and a businesswoman, said she liked me a lot. She claimed that when she was in Cameroon for business, my name was brought to the desks of various businessmen for pleasure. (Beat)

"To them," in her words, "your name represented the pleasure every man seeks."

She told me that she wished I was into women. (Pause)
I had never even thought about it before, but it didn't seem like a bad idea. One thing led to another. (Pause)
It was my first time engaging in homosexuality. It was then that I became a lesbian. From then onwards, men didn't matter to me. (Beat)
My business with them was purely professional, and that was it. Though I was living with Michel in his Paris home, I looked forward to a time when I could finally leave him and join Marie. (Beat)
I had money, so that wasn't a problem. In fact, I was richer than Michel! I asked him in a roundabout way, what he hated, and found out he detested lesbians. (Beat)
So, I arranged with Marie to come to my place to do it about the same time Michel came home from work. And that's how he found out. (Beat)
That was the end of Michel's and my relationship and the beginning of what I thought would be the pleasure of life from another dimension. (Pause)
Marie asked me to join the group she was a member of in Paris. She called it "The Sisters Seeking Extra Pleasure".
According to her, the group guaranteed each member great fortunes, provided then engaged in mixed sexualities, bestiality, homosexuality, simultaneous multiple sexes with same of opposite sex, marathon

sex, and extreme sex situations. (Beat)

The more the member did this, the more the material returns. That got me interested! I signed up with the organization to the tune of $10,000. And I became a member. (Pause) The members were told that they had to attend monthly meetings. Before I could go professional with my trade, I had to practice the acts for fun before I could see the monetary gains. (Beat)

I have engaged in various sex acts; bestiality, lesbianism, group sex, marathon sex. The list is endless! The harsh truth is that, because of these choices, my sexuality status was entirely affected. (Beat)

I couldn't make up my mind what I enjoyed more; the sexual companionship of a man, fellow woman, or animal. But my saving grace was that before I engaged in any of the acts, I never had sex with anything without the use of condoms. (Beat)

Therefore, HIV/AIDS, Syphilis, Gonorrhea, Staph, and any other STD have never been found on me. Interestingly, since my stay in prison I'm very surprised that the urge to have you ladies has never even crossed my mind! (Pause)

A month later, I got to the meeting venue only to realize that it was actually a warehouse! When I asked the manager of the place, he told me he'd never heard of my friends and that such a group didn't exist there. (Pause)

I knew I'd been duped! I had to look for

Marie the best way I could because all I had now was less than $5,000! After a long period of time, I got to realize that the name she gave me was actually the name of a deceased female politician in Paris. (Beat)

She was a scammer who needed to be tracked. Through my research, I found that she was in fact, French-South African, and that she was living in Johannesburg. (Beat)

I was determined to have my pound of flesh from her. (Pause)

I went back to Michel, demanding a sum of $10,000. I knew he could afford it. Now married and with two kids, he gave me the money, but with a firm warning: "don't come anywhere near me or my family." (Pause)

I traveled to South Africa and got the exact address where Marie lived. As she came to the door, she was surprised to see that it was me. (Beat)

She tried to run away but I caught her and beat her until she was black-and-blue and was almost dead. It took the intervention of neighbors to rescue her. (Pause)

Unfortunately, Marie gave up the ghost on the hospital bed. By that time, of course, the police had been called, and I was arrested. (Beat)

I was charged by the court for accidental murder and battery. The court considered the case files of the deceased into the charge; as she was a wanted criminal in South Africa, the verdict was reduced.

(Beat)
Instead of sentencing me to life in prison, which was normal I would be given a 15 and ½ year prison sentence.

MAMA You've heard our stories. Now it's your turn. As you can see, we want to hear your story. All of this will help up to live in hope as we serve our jail terms.

MAYA I am Maya Isaacs. Born to Samuel Isaacs and a woman, who, according to my father, was named Cynthia. I am the only child of my father. (Beat)
Born and bred in Durban and raised by a single father, my life was incomplete. I had quality primary and secondary school education. (Beat)
But my quest for knowing who I really am, what I termed "destiny", kept me distracted from the reality of how caring my dad was. (Pause)
It was in my pursuit for destiny that I ran into a certain Craig who introduced me to a society for juveniles called the Alternative Lifestyle Club. (Beat)
I was told by the leader that if I wanted to achieve my aim in this life of mine, I would have to ensure that my father and I no longer lived together. (Beat)
Despite the detailed story my father told me about myself, I was skeptical. So, instead, I followed the counsel of the ALC. I also endured the torture of the initiation rites. (Beat)

That's a long story in itself! So, I provoked my father to anger, who consequently beat me to a pulp. And as planned, I called Ms. Diana's number, and she came to my residence, in the company of her close confidant, Craig, and police. (Beat)

They arrested my dad and had me taken to the hospital. The verdict by the Durban Magistrate Court favored my freedom. It was then that I moved in with Craig and completed my education. (Pause)

I was given 3 assignments with dates all specified; drug trafficking in the form of courier services to various destinations, prostitution, and robbery. (Beat)

It was on one of these assignments that I shot the famous merchant, Van Brussels. I peddled drugs successfully as instructed, and was regular jump-around material. (Beat)

The prince of Swaziland was one of the numerous clients I dealt with. But I felt something was fishy. Craig, my assigned guardian, was not giving me my money when due. (Beat)

I asked him a number of times, but he kept giving me the same vague answers. To me, enough was enough! I decided to do things my own way. (Beat)

The ALC decided to disclose me to the police on my last drug peddling trip to Johannesburg. I was arrested in 2001, charged for attempted murder and drug trafficking, and sentenced to 3 years in

prison. (Beat)
I haven't seen my father since! What a mistake!

MONTAGE
Maya reading.
Maya sitting in the lotus position with her eyes closed.
Maya smiling with the others in her cell.
Maya speaking to a few inmates in a courtyard. Maya reading.
Maya speaking to a larger group of inmates in a courtyard.
END MONTAGE

Scene 77
INT: PRISON DINING HALL – DAY
A wall calendar indicates it's January 8, 2002.
Many inmates, jailers, and civilians are present. Van Brussels, in a wheelchair, is by the last table. Maya comes to the podium.

MAYA   Our minds, based on what the five sense perceive reveal to us our personalities; the way we approach issues. (Beat)
In this world of increasing materialistic cravings, humanity craves the physical dimensions its natural senses are in tune with. (Beat)
Getting good cars, connections in high places, clothes, making money, building great structures, and aspiring to outclass everyone are the goals much of mankind has
successfully attained. But attaining them

came with a price! (Pause)

Killings, prostitution, drug trafficking, and other vices are often the means to that end. Hence, the reason world crimes have seriously increased. (Beat)

Not only am I the physical prisoner you see. Like many, I am also a prisoner of my own fight for those goals. Our bodily desires have limited our access to the infinite potential our Creator has bestowed on us. (Pause)

Until we free our minds of mental slavery, we forever remain imprisoned. Just as we, the prisoners are under check by the wardens or jailers, so are we all, imprisoned by the knowledge we have, checked by the wardens and 5 senses. (Beat)

Until we are free from the greed and materialism our senses put us under, and instead strive for what our Creator intended, we will remain imprisoned, no matter where we are physically. (Pause)

In finishing, I would like to emphasize this. If we don't emancipate ourselves from mental slavery, individually, our reality at the end of the day will be like this saying. A man with determination but no conception is like reaching a destination without intention. (Pause) Thanks for listening!

The inmates give enthusiastic applause. Khadijah, Mercy, and Mama congratulate Maya. Inmates and jailers line up and congratulate Maya.

Scene 78

INT: PRISON DINING HALL – DAY
A few prisoners are left in the line to congratulate Maya. Van Brussels wheels to the end of the line.
The others congratulate Maya. Van Brussels is before Maya. Maya appears stunned. Maya falls to her knees and cries as she places her hands on his thigh.

MAYA   I'm sorry for what I did to you. (Beat) It was what I was told to do by Ms. Diana through the ALC!

VAN BRUSSELS   (Gentle Voice) I know Maya. (Beat) Even when you shot me, I knew you had what it takes to be the great woman you are becoming. If not for the wickedness of Ms. Diana and her cohorts, you wouldn't be here in the first place. (Beat)

You should know that investigations are going on regarding Ms. Diana's ALC's criminal activities, herself, my aide Henry Yale, and other conspirators. (Beat)

Henry Yale confessed to me after being arrested that he worked with Ms. Diana to give you the opportunity to do what you never wanted to do. I could tell that the shooting was not your idea, because my powers of intuition said so, and they have never failed me! (Beat)

Rest assured, my dear, justice will bring them to trial! More importantly, you will be released within the next 3 months…That, I promise you. I'll use my connections in our government to get you out of this prison. (Beat)

You are too precious to spend even 6 months

here. You weren't guilty at all, because you were only being taken advantage of. I just happened to be the victim. (Beat)
You'll be vindicated, and I will make sure that you won't be held responsible for any crime. I'm behind you, I promise!

MAYA That will be wonderful, sir! (Beat) I owe you one, sir!

VAN BRUSSELS Mark my words, within the next 3 months you will be out of here.

Scene 79
INT: JAIL CELL - DAY
The calendar shows May 31, 2002. There are footsteps. Maya cries as she hugs, Khadijah, Mama, and Mercy.

MAYA I will miss you all big time! But be assured, I will come back to get you all released!

The Jailor opens the cell door. Maya steps out of the cell.

MAMA I believe in you. I have no doubt that you will come for us! We are looking forward to seeing you soon.

Scene 80
INT: JAIL CORRIDOR - DAY
CUT TO:
Maya's former cellmates, and the other prisoners, wave to her.

Scene 81
EXT: JAIL - DAY
Maya, wearing a fashionable and upscale outfit, with Van Brussels and people in dark suits and glasses, walks out the

front door.

Scene 82
EXT: A MANSION - DAY
A limousine drives to the mansion's front door.
A man in a dark suit and glasses steps out of the limousine.
Van Brussels, then Maya step out of the limousine.

Scene 83
INT: STUDY - DAY
Maya is sitting in a chair. Van Brussels hands Maya a piece of paper. Van Brussels sits in a chair.

MAYA
Dear Maya. (Beat) It is a pleasure to inform you that you have been given a work permit to study Secretarial Studies, and to work at the Louisville Institute of Secretarial Studies and Louisville Shipping Company with a monthly salary of $5,000. (Beat)
We look forward to your answer indicating your interest. (Beat) Yours Faithfully, (Beat) Van Brussels, (Beat) Chairman, (Beat) Louisville Shipping Company. (Pause)
Thank you so much for this great opportunity. I'm very happy that this is happening to me, especially after all that has happened. I promise to be the best I can be. No disappointments! (Beat) I guarantee you excellence at school and work.

VAN BRUSSELS
I know you'll make me proud. Going by what you talked about on that day when I saw you at the prison, Louisville will know that Maya can stand up to anybody,

	anytime, and anywhere. (Beat) I hope you have a great experience. You need not thank me! You deserve what you're being offered, even more! (Pause) By the way. (Beat) Do you have a Secondary School Leaving Certificate?
MAYA	Yes! (Beat) I have an Advanced Level Cambridge GCE, which I sat in my school, St. Steven Beak Comprehensive College, Durban.
VAN BRUSSELS	Do you mind my driver taking you there?
MAYA	I don't mind sir.

MONTAGE:
Maya steps out of a limousine at Durban International Airport.
A South African Airways Boeing 747 takes off.
A Terminal sign reads "Baton Rouge Metropolitan Airport".
A man in a suit leads Maya into a limousine as a chauffer puts Maya's bags in the trunk.
The Limousine drives onto the Louisville Institute of Secretarial Studies campus.
END MONTAGE:

Scene 84
INT: MAYA'S APARTMENT - DAY
The apartment is spacious. The living room has a sofa. It has a bookcase filled with books. There is a dining area with a refrigerator. Maya is at a desktop computer. The computer dings. "You've got mail."
There are a couple of mouse clicks. There's an email from Van Brussels. "Subject: Final Grades" A double click. An

email opens.
"How did you do on the finals?" *The pointer moves to "reply". There's a click. keystrokes.*
"My GPA is 4.50." *The pointer moves to "send". There's a click.*

Scene 85
INT: LIVING ROOM – DAY
Van Brussels is at his laptop.

VAN BRUSSELS
ON SCREEN: A Grade Point Average of 4.5. I knew she could do it. (Beat) I'd better get her on contract before someone else does.

Scene 86
INT: MAYA'S APARTMENT – DAY
There's a KNOCK at the door. Maya opens it.
DANIEL YOUNG, handsome, papers in hand, is at the door.

DANIEL I'm Daniel Young, General Manager of the Louisville Shipping Company. (Beat) My boss, Van Brussels, instructed me to talk to you about signing the agreement contract I have with me. He told me about you and wants you to sign it before I leave. (Beat)
In fact, Van Brussels instructed that the agreement be signed 3 weeks before your final examination.

Maya grins.
MAYA Come in, Daniel.
Daniel steps inside.
MAYA Please, make yourself comfortable!
Maya gestures at the sofa. Daniel sits

DANIEL   Thanks.
MAYA   Can I get you something? (Beat) I have quite a lot of fruit juices in the house, natural fruits, frozen chicken, Swiss cheese, hamburgers, Dr. Pepper, and a lot of other things. Just order and I will deliver!
DANIEL   No, thank you, Maya. (Beat) I'm not hungry. All I want is for you to sign the agreement document.
Daniel hands Maya the papers. Maya looks over the document.
MAYA   Let me get my pen. It's in my bag.
Maya steps away.
DANIEL   That won't be necessary. I have one with me already.
MAYA   Anything else? Sure, you won't have something before you go?
Maya opens the refrigerator. Daniel shakes his head and smiles.
DANIEL   Okay. (Beat) Before I go, let me have a Dr. Pepper. For your sake, I'll have two.
Maya grins. She takes 2 Dr. Peppers out of the refrigerator and hands them to Daniel.
DANIEL   My attention is needed at the office. I will see you some other time. And I wish you all the best in your examinations, Maya. It's nice to have met you.
Daniel steps towards the door.
MAYA   I'm looking forward to knowing you better.

Scene 87
INT: A LARGE AUDITORIUM – DAY
The graduates in their caps and gowns stand in line. Maya

is next to accept her diploma. Friends and relatives sit in the mezzanine and balcony. The SPEAKER, wearing a cap and gown, is at the podium.

SPEAKER   Maya Isaacs, Summa Cum Laude.
Maya walks across the stage and accepts her diploma and a handshake from the principal.

EXT: A BUILDING – DAY
Daniel Young is with two OTHERS.

DAINEL   Congratulations. Summa Cum Laude. A great accomplishment.
He shakes Maya's hand.
OTHER 1   Congratulations.
Shakes Maya's hand.
OTHER 2   Congratulations.
Shakes Maya's hand.
DAINEL   Mr. Van Brussels is in town and is looking forward to seeing you.
She takes pictures with some of her fellow graduates.

Scene 88
INT: AN OFFICE BUILDING – DAY
A SUPERVISOR leads Maya to a cubicle.

SUPERVISOR   This is your cubicle. Welcome aboard.

Scene 89
INT: AN AUDITORIUM – DAY
Daniel, with a few subordinates, is at the front of the auditorium. The employees are seated.

DANIEL   The Employee of the Year, for the second year in a row. Is Maya Isaacs.

The employees applaud. A subordinate gives Daniel a plaque. Maya makes her way to Daniel.

Scene 90
INT: A BOARD ROOM – DAY
Van Brussels sits with the other BOARD MEMBERS.

BOARD MEMBER   Next item is Van Brussels' recommendation to promote Maya Isaacs to the position of an assistant to the General Secretary, Henry Racks. All in favor?

All hands raise.

BOARD MEMBER   Motion carries.

Scene 91
INT: AN OFFICE BUILDING – DAY
MAYA Walks to her cubicle. She sees an envelope on her keyboard. Maya opens the envelope and reads.

DANIEL YOUNG (O.C.)   Dear Maya. (Beat) We, the staff members of Louisville Shipping Company hereby congratulate you on your birthday! Happy Birthday, Maya! (Pause)
You have been an indefatigable instrument for the growth of this company. Your commitment, transparency, accountability, relational abilities, and honesty have singled you out among your colleagues. (Beat)
Louisville Shipping Company is proud to have you in its workforce. You are an indispensable asset. (Pause)

> To this effect, we have agreed to raise your level of responsibility from Trainee Secretary to Assistant Secretary. Within the next 48 hours you will become assistant to the General Secretary, Henry Racks. (Pause)
> We would like to hear what you have to say about your promotion. Your presence is requested at the Board of Directors meeting, and it is a direct order from Van Brussels, who will be here to witness your decision. (Pause)
> We hope that this promotion will motivate you to even greater productivity, in order to continue the progress of this company. Please take this letter to the office of the General Manager, affirming that you have accepted. He will issue documents that you will need to sign. (Pause)
> Once again, congratulations on your birthday and promotion. (Pause) Daniel Young, General Manager.

Maya has a big smile as she strolls out of her office.

Scene 92
INT: GENERAL MANAGER'S OFFICE – DAY
Maya and Daniel are smiling as Daniel puts a series of papers in front of her, which Maya dutifully signa.

Scene 93
INT: MAYA'S APARTMENT – DAY
Maya enters. She has a big smile and dances with excitement. Her demeanor becomes serious.

MAYA (Whispers) Is my father still alive? (Normal voice) Since he didn't bother looking for me, I won't go looking for him. I will go ahead with my life, because I have found the life I ought to be living!

Scene 94
INT: A BOARD ROOM – DAY
The 12 members of the executive board are around a large table. HENRY RACKS and Daniel are there. Maya puts on a wireless microphone.

MAYA First of all, I would like to thank you all for this wonderful opportunity to speak to such distinguished ladies and gentlemen. I would like to express my heartfelt gladness for your kindness in promoting me to the position of Assistant to the General Secretary of this company. (Pause)
It is a great honor to be given this privilege to expand my level of responsibility. Under the watchful eyes of my mentors, Van Brussels Daniel Young, and Henry Racks, I was able to excel in my previous position as Trainee Secretary. (Beat)
With the existing working relationship among us all, I am sure of making this company proud wherever I go. If not for your cooperation as a team, I do not think I would have climbed to this height. (Beat)
You made me what I am today, not me. I want to use this opportunity to say a big "thank you" for making this a possibility. (Pause)

>   With this newly attained position, I promise to give my best to make this company one of the top-notch outfits in the world. Together, we can make this pursuit attainable. (Pause) Once again, I want to thank you for taking time off from your busy schedules to come listen to me. Your presence here gives me the motivation to give the best of quality services to our esteemed clients. (Pause)
>   I leave you with one of my favorite quotes: "In the pursuit of peace, liberty, and life we stand, and in God we trust." (Pause)
>   Thank you for listening!

The board gives a round of applause.
The board members stand and shake hands with Maya.
Van Brussels gives Maya a hug.
Daniel gives Maya a peck on both cheeks.
Maya appears pleasantly surprised by Daniel's kisses.

Scene 95
INT: OUTSIDE HENRY RACKS' OFFICE – DAY
Maya is typing at her desk. Henry Racks steps outside his office.

HENRY   I've never seen such a dedicated employee in all my years working for this company.

MAYA   Thank you.

Henry Racks exits.

Scene 96
INT: BREAK AREA – DAY
Maya enters and walks to the water cooler. As Maya is pouring water Daniel enters.

DANIEL   Maya, I was wondering if you would want to go to dinner with me after work?
MAYA   No, I really can't I have a lot to do so I have to work late and come in early tomorrow.

Scene 97
INT: LUNCH ROOM – DAY
Maya and Daniel are eating lunch together.

DANIEL   Could we go out together tomorrow?
MAYA   No, I have so much work I have to work through the weekend.

Scene 98
INT: BREAK AREA – DAY
Maya is leaving the break room as Daniel walks in.

DANIEL   Maya, would you want to come with me to The Louisville Bar after work.
MAYA   Yes, why not.

Scene 99
INT: THE LOUISVILLE BAR – DAY
Daniel and Maya sit opposite each other. A SERVER comes to their table.

SERVER   What are you having?
DANIEL   A Dr. Pepper for me. (Beat) Maya?
MAYA   Do you have a sweet non-alcoholic wine?
SERVER   Yes, we do.

Scene 100
INT: THE LOUISVILLE BAR – LATER – DAY
Daniel and Maya's glasses are about ½ full.

DANIEL: Maya, I'd like to get to know you on a more personal level. Every since I met you, to be candid, I've been feeling something I'd never felt in my entire life. What do you say?

MAYA: What else do you want to know about me? I'm Maya Isaacs, the assistant secretary of Louisville Shipping Company, a graduate of the institute of secretarial studies. I think that's all you need to know about me.

Daniel takes a sip of his soda.

DANIEL: That's really not enough. I would like to know your background, family, life relationships, ambitions in life, and so on.

Maya looks down at her glass. She sighs. She pushes her glass away.

MAYA: I have learned from experience that if your past doesn't help your present, then dump it and move on with your life to enjoy a better future. (Beat)

However, I have also come to embrace the harsh reality that there are some certain past events that will forever stay with us, no matter how hard we try to dump them. (Beat)

In fact, they are part of what makes us who we are. All we need do is to endeavor to manage them or better yet, learn to live with them. As you've already known, I go by the name Maya Isaacs. (Beat)

I was raised by a single father, by the name

of Samuel Isaacs. According to what he told me he divorced my mother on grounds of infidelity before I reached the age of 3. (Beat)
South African by nationality and Durban by origin, I attended the St. John's Baptist Primary School and Steven Beak Comprehensive College, all in Durban. (Beat)
Before completing my secondary school education, I felt my dad wasn't telling me the whole story, the real reason that actually led to his divorcing his wife. (Beat)
So, in pursuit of what I called my destiny, I ran into a certain guy named Craig who introduced me to the Alternative Lifestyle Club, and organization based in Durban, South Africa whose supposed aim was to give juveniles, especially the ones from broken homes, a life that they didn't have living with their single parents. (Pause)
One thing led to the other and my life was changed forever, negatively I might add, until I me Van Brussels. (Beat) If I go on telling the whole story, we won't leave this place. For more information about me, you can visit my blog. Would you like the link?

DANIEL Absolutely.

Daniel takes out his cellphone.

MAYA www.maya.blogspot.com.

Daniel types into his cellphone.

MAYA At this point, it is my turn to know who this Prince Charming is who is talking to me.

Daniel puts away his phone.

DANIEL   Unfortunately, when I was 5, my parents died in a plane crash. My parents were good friends with Van Brussels when they were at the University of Pretoria in South Africa. (Beat)

In fact, he told me he would have wanted to marry my mom, but Frank was her choice of man. After their death, Van Brussels adopted me as his son. (Pause)

I lived only partly in South Africa. Since he had no children with his wife, who died of ALS, he took me as his only child. (Beat)

By then, he had founded the Louisville Institute of Secretarial Studies and Louisville Shipping Company, and owned great shares in the South African gold-mining fields. (Beat)

When I was 18, I was sent to University of Texas to study business management, and then to Harvard School of Business for my Masters. (Beat)

I intend to enroll in a Doctorate program in Strategic Business Planning at Oxford University in London soon. As for relationships, I have not been into any serious ones. (Beat)

But now, however, I want to settle down. And that's for real! To prove a point, I'll be searching through the internet articles that convey the ways to marrying the right woman. (Beat)

I'm hoping to find a match on one of those dating websites. (Pause) There's only one thing keeping me from seriously following this path, and it's Van Brussels' disability. (Beat)

Did you ever hear how he ended up in a wheelchair? (Beat)

Can you believe that he was shot and left to die? Of course, he didn't die, but the shooting left him lame for the rest of his life. (Beat) I can't get over the anger, and I don't understand why he doesn't say who shot him. I ask him once in a while but he won't disclose who that person was!

Tears roll down Maya's cheeks.

DANIEL	What's wrong Maya?
MAYA	Can we leave this place, Daniel?
DANIEL	Have I offended you, Maya? Tell me, should I change to another topic? What can I do to show that I love you?

Maya's eyes widen.

MAYA	You're joking right? (Pause) Did I hear you almost say, "what can I do to show that I love you? Do you mean what you are saying?
DANIEL	Y-yes-
MAYA	IF you claim you love me, take me home to my apartment while you go your way! But please, visit that website. (Beat) I won't be available tomorrow, so please don't try to contact me. And please, don't ask me what I'll be doing!
DANIEL	I'll do as you've said, Maya. But don't expect me to just leave things like this.

Scene 101
EXT: MAYA'S APARTMENT BUILDING – NIGHT

Daniel's car stops in front and Maya steps out.

Scene 102
INT: DANIEL'S APARTMENT - NIGHT
The door opens. Daniel steps in and turns on a light. He steps to his computer and presses the power button.

Scene 103
INT: MAYA'S APARTMENT - NIGHT
Maya appears nervous as she paces back and forth.

Scene 104
INT: DANIEL'S APARTMENT - NIGHT
Daniel sits by his computer. He types on the keyboard. He impatiently watches the monitor. He reads what's on the screen. His expression changes from shock, to horror, to rage. Daniel rushes to his telephone. He puts his hand on the phone then backs away.

Scene 105
INT: MAYA'S BEDROOM - NIGHT
Maya is sleeping. The air conditioner is the only sound. The phone rings. Maya, groggy, looks at the telephone number display. Maya hesitates, then clicks on the speaker.

MAYA (Hesitant) Daniel?

DANIEL (O.C.) Maya, I know you're afraid of what would happen when I read your story. But please, don't worry. What has happened has happened! It was a shock at first, I must admit. But I understand. (Pause)
Admittedly, I felt unhappy while I read through the whole story. But when I gave it a

re-think, I realized that it wasn't deliberate. (Beat)

Because of your naiveté you did something that you really didn't want to do. I am sorry for what has happened to you through the years. (Pause)

You probably thought I'd never have you as part of my life again. On the contrary, I would like to see you not only as my friend and lover if you permit me, but my confidante! (Beat)

What you've gone through is more than enough reason to make me love you the more!

MAYA (Crying) Do you know that I am celibate? But from this day onward, Daniel, I am forever yours! You still want to be with me despite my rough past! (Beat) I'm forever grateful. God bless the day I met you!

DANIEL (O.C.) (Chuckles) One step at a time, my dear! (Beat) I'm happy things are about working out between us. It's all that matters!

MAYA Okay, Yes, I agree.

DANIEL (O.C.) From the look of things, I'm seeing that I have hmmm found my wife from among so many women.

MAYA Who could that be?

DANIEL (O.C.) It's the woman speaking with me! (Beat) Maya, you became the other half of my heart the first day I set eyes on you. I realized you'd be the woman I'd wanted. A woman of truth, love, and humbleness. (Beat)

Right from the first time I saw you, it was

crystal clear that you were the only one. Only if you could say "yes", I'll never forget this moment.

Maya grows a big smile, then closes her eyes. There is a long silence.

MAYA　　　　　Yes! I'll be your wife. Oh, Daniel, I feel the same way! Since the first time I set my eyes on you, when you came to my apartment during my final year in school, I knew you'd be my husband. (Beat) This is the happiest day of my life. God bless the day I met you!

There is laughing over the speaker. Maya joins in the laughter.

DANIEL (O.C.)　(Serious) Now that you're unofficially my wife, I would like to see what I can do to take away the burden of your past. Is there anything I can do?

MAYA　　　　　I don't know. (Beat) I wouldn't know where to start.

DANIEL (O.C.)　Perhaps you could start by telling me what your greatest worry is. As we discussed earlier, we all have the bags and baggage of our past coming along with us in the journey of marriage we are starting.

MAYA　　　　　To me, my greatest worry is where my father is. It's been about 10 years since I last saw him. I've been in search of him in my own way but it has been interrupted a lot. (Beat)
Coupled with my very busy work schedule, I rarely have been able to devote time for this fully. (Pause)
I'll have to intensify my search for him by

creating time. Or what do you think, my dear?

DANIEL (O.C.)   I said I'd help you and I will my dear. I've signed up for this challenge! Together, we'll find him, I'm sure. We'll make the time for this.

MAYA   Honey, you are getting tired. It's about 3:30 AM and we've been on the phone for over an hour. To be frank, I'm tired as well. Sweetheart, I would like some sleep but I'll stay on and talk if you want.

DANIEL (O.C.)   Who am I to disturb you from sleeping? I'm also tired and need to get to bed. (Yawns) This is as well the happiest moment of my life! Go get some sleep, sweetheart! Wishing you a happy Sunday! I look forward to seeing you at work!

MAYA   I wish you the same, Daniel. Multiple kisses from me to you! I love you!

Maya KISSES at the phone.

DANIEL (O.C.)   I love you too!

Scene 106
INT: OUTSIDE HENRY RACKS'S OFFICE – DAY
The wall clock shows 8:30. Maya arrives at her desk.
There is an envelope on her keyboard. The envelope reads "For your eyes only, Maya. From Daniel." Maya tears the envelope open and reads the letter.

DANIEL (O.C.)   It's good that life has united the sun and moon together in an atmosphere of love, sealed the stars with the haziness of affection, heightened the green shoots of peace, surrounding it with the waters of

endurance. (Pause)
What I mean to say, my precious pearl, is that I thank you for giving me the key to unlocking the softest spot in your heart. (Beat)
The place that no man has ever had access to. I promise to love you as long as I live. I love you too much to ever let harm come to you. (Pause)
I was so carried away by your aura of greatness, the very grace you carry. I am happy to be a partaker of this great virtue. (Beat)
Please, my true love, from the bottom of my heart to the depth of my soul, do not be offended by my short words the other night. It was just that I couldn't help thinking about you all the time, and so my attention was distracted from the conversation. (Pause) Frankly, you're an epitome of joy, Maya. (Pause) God bless the very day I met you! (Pause) From Daniel, (Pause) Your sweetheart.

Maya presses the letter to her chest.

Scene 107
INT: MAYA'S APARTMENT - NIGHT
Maya has a box full of items as the walks out the door.

Scene 108
INT: DANIEL'S APARTMENT - NIGHT
Daniel opens the door. Maya is outside the door with a box full of things. Daniel takes it off her hands.

Scene 109
EXT: MAYA'S APARTMENT COMPLEX – DAY
Maya and Daniel put a piece of furniture into Daniel's car. The car is loaded with furniture and household items.

Scene 110
INT: DANIEL'S APARTMENT – NIGHT
Maya and Daniel carry a piece of furniture inside.

Scene 111
EXT: LOUSIVILLE WATER PARK – DAY
Chairs are set up in a large field of grass. The chairs are facing a river. Opposite are the Water Tower buildings. There is an American flag at ½ staff. The guests are seated. The OFFICIANT, Daniel and Maya stand under the arch.

OFFICIANT By the power vested in me by the State of Louisiana I now pronounce you husband and wife.

The guests applaud. The guests stand and make their way to congratulate the newlyweds.
GUEST 1 takes notice of something in the distance.

GUEST 1 Why is that flag only half way up.
GUEST 2 It's November 11, an American holiday.
GUEST 1 Strange.
GUEST 2 Where are they going for their honeymoon?
GUEST 1 Paris, they'll leave tomorrow and come back a week after the New Year.
GUEST 2 Sounds wonderful.

Scene 112

INT: OFFICE DOOR - DAY
There is an envelope taped to the door that reads "Maya". Maya approaches the door. She takes the envelope off the door.

Scene 113
INT: ANOTHER OFFICE DOOR - DAY
There is an envelope taped to the door that reads "Daniel". Daniel approaches the door. He takes the envelope off the door.

Scene 114
EXT: HOTEL - DAY
The sign on the hotel reads, "Manihot Hotels and Suites". Daniel and Maya approach the hotel.

Scene 115
INT: HOTEL SUITE - DAY
Daniel and Maya enter. Van Brussels and Henry Racks are in the suite.

VAN BRUSSELS   Congratulations to the newest couple in town! How was your honeymoon in Paris?

Daniel and Maya sit. They hold hands. Daniel rests their hands, on his lap.

DANIEL   A great one it was!

VAN BRUSSELS   Good! I'm glad to hear that! (Beat) Now to the business of the day. I called both of you here to let you know that you will be leaving for South Africa to head my branch.

Daniel appears stunned.

VAN BRUSSELS   I'm sorry, son, for not letting

you know about this 5-year plan. This secret was just between Henry Racks and me. (Pause)
Daniel, you will be the Chief Executive Officer of the South African branch of Louisville Shipping Company, while you, Maya, will be the General Secretary. (Beat)
To that effect, here are the necessary documents with your names on them and necessary signatures for authentication purposes. (Pause)
Maya, you've been tested and you have shown yourself trustworthy, and that is the reason you've been given this position. (Pause)
Operations have started and the employees there have been notified. All they're waiting for is your arrival. You'll be leaving in the next 2 weeks, so get your things packed. (Beat)
Your visas will be available within the next 48 hours. The earlier you prepare for this journey the better. (Pause)
Son, you and Maya will have to manage my shares in the major South African gold mines.

Van Brussels appears tired.
VAN BRUSSELS   I'm getting older and weaker by the day.

MONTAGE:
A hotel conference room has a "Farewell Daniel & Maya" banner.
Daniel and Maya smile as the guests shake hands with

them.
A Republic of South Africa 747 lands.
Daniel and Maya exit the Durban IAP terminal.
END MONTAGE:

Scene 116
INT: LIMOSINE – DRIVING – DAY
Daniel and Maya are in the back. Daniel takes in the car view of Durban.

DANIEL	It's great to be back in South Africa.
MAYA	Yes, it is great. (Pause) On top of everything else it gives me a good opportunity to locate my father. (Pause) I am ambivalent about finding him. I want to see him again, but I don't know how he will react to seeing me.
DANIEL	I understand your feelings. (Beat) Either way things work out for the best. All will be fine.

Scene 117
INT: THE YOUNG'S HOME – DAY
Daniel and Maya are in the living room.

DANIEL	We have been here a month. I think it's time for us to search for your father in earnest.
MAYA	Yes, you are right.
DANIEL	We will take a 2-day leave of absence and in that time, we will do nothing but search for your father.
MAYA	That is a wonderful idea.

Scene 118
EXT: SAMUEL'S OLD HOUSE – DAY
The house has some changes from when Maya seen it last. A car drive to the house. Maya and Daniel, wearing a T-shirt, steps out of the car.

MAYA
The house seems to have changed a little from the way it used to be. Well, things change.

Maya shrugs and walks to the house. Daniel follows her. Maya knocks on the door. A WOMAN opens the door.

WOMAN
Who are you?

MAYA
I'm Maya Young, and behind me is my husband, Daniel.

WOMAN
Well, what do you want?

MAYA
My maiden name is Maya Isaacs. This was the house where my father, Samuel Isaacs live in."

WOMAN
I'm very sorry! Pardon me for my impoliteness. I didn't know who you were. (Beat) He was such a nice man!

MAYA
What do you mean "he was such a nice man"?

Maya takes Daniel's hand. Daniel puts his other hand on Maya's shoulder.

WOMAN
Yes. (Beat) Your father did a lot of good for me! He was the one who gave me this house at a give-away price, under the condition that I give a note to one Maya Isaacs, whenever she came to this place again. (Beat) I've been living here for the past 5 years. (Pause)
Two weeks after he relinquished ownership of the house to me, the

                        neighborhood's security alerted me that
                        Samuel had shot himself in the head.
MAYA   What? No!
Maya cries.
MAYA   What, what happened? Where did
                        they? What did they do with him?
David holds Maya close. Woman has a look of pity.
WOMAN   Where his body was taken to, I don't
                        know. This happened around the month of
                        December of 2003. I've made serious
                        inquiries about it, but the authorities say
                        that he has been buried according to the
                        Suicidal Law, which means that the corpse
                        belongs to the government. Therefore, no
                        one can lay claims to it.
The woman looks away as tears flow down Maya's cheeks.
WOMAN   Let me go inside the house to get the
                        note.
Maya continues crying and Daniel continues trying to comfort her. The woman comes to the door with an envelope in hand.
WOMAN   This is the note he wrote. Your name
                        was written on its seal. You can now have it,
                        Maya.
Maya takes the envelope. She opens the envelope and takes out the letter.
MAYA   Dear Maya, (Pause) It's been a long
                        time since you left me to live in this world
                        alone. I wanted to tell you who you really
                        were at the right time, but your impatient
                        and sudden change in character led you
                        astray and out of my reach. (Beat)
                        Initially, I thought of disowning you
                        because of your unruly behavior towards

me, but the love I had for you changed my mind. (Pause)

To be candid, I had tried through the years you were with me to hide the harsh reality that I'm not your biological father. Gat, Cynthia's lover, impregnated her during their illicit affair. (Beat)

I knew about this but couldn't help matters because of the love I had for her. I also know it is true because of the fact that I'm medically impotent, meaning that I can't father a child. (Beat)

I lost my manhood's potency to an accident at the age of 25. (Pause)

It had been a long time since I'd last seen Gat and Cynthia. So, I decided to use my contacts to invite Gat and Cynthia to know who their daughter was, and to introduce you to them as your biological parents. (Beat)

Unfortunately, I found out that they were both dead. The cause of their death, at the time of this writing, November 2, 2003, remains unknown to me. (Pause)

Maya, the world had been miserable to me. I have made arrangements to procure a pistol to kill myself. Therefore, by the time you read this, if ever, I will have been long gone. (Pause)

But one thing I want to assure you is this. I will always love you, my daughter! (Pause)

Your Daddy, Samuel.

Maya cries harder. The woman and Daniel try to console her.

MAYA   Why me? (Beat) I have lost my dad because of my behavior! Why, Maya? Why?

DANIEL   Don't worry, honey. (Beat) You still have me and my dad. We've been with you all this time and you're a part of our family.

Maya looks at Daniel. Maya notices Daniel's T-shirt stained with her tears and mascara. Daniel looks at his T-shirt.

DANIEL   Don't worry about that either.

Two children inside the house are making indistinct noise.

WOMAN   (Whispers) I'm so very sorry.

She turns to Daniel.

WOMAN   I'm sorry, but I have to go.

Daniel nods.

DANIEL   (Whispers) Thank you.

The woman goes inside the house and closes the door. Maya looks at the sky.

MAYA   This date, marked December 19, 2008, I have made a vow to celebrate you unlike any other. I will celebrate it like I do Christmas and other festive seasons. Daddy, be assured that as long as I live on earth, I will live up to the promise! (Shouting) I love you, Daddy!

Daniel nods agreement.

FADE OUT:

THE END

www.ingramcontent.com/pod-product-compliance
Lightning Source LLC
Chambersburg PA
CBHW072011290426
44109CB00018B/2204